SPORT
COMMUNICATION

AN INTERPERSONAL APPROACH
DARIELA RODRIGUEZ

Kendall Hunt
publishing company

D0140580

Cover image © Lori Sullivan Photography

Kendall Hunt
publishing company

www.kendallhunt.com
Send all inquiries to:
4050 Westmark Drive
Dubuque, IA 52004-1840

DEDICATION

I would like to thank my family for their support through this
process and so much more. Kimberly, Mom, Dad, Marilisa, Mark, Mia, and Marlee . . .
you all make the hard work easier everyday.

BRIEF CONTENTS

TABLE OF CONTENTS

PREFACE

THEORY AND COMMUNICATION

The goal of this book is to explain just how intricate the relationships in sports can be from a multitude of different perspectives. When most individuals think about sports based relationships, the first one that comes to mind is the coach-athlete relationship. This is the one that is most prevalent in people's minds because it is the one consistently shown on television. Be it displayed in movies, television shows, or broadcasts of sporting events, the coach-athlete relationship gets a lot of attention. More recently, the parent and athlete relationship has gained increased attention as the behaviors of the members of the Millennial generation are usually directly linked to one or both of their "helicopter parents".

Though these relationships are often at the forefront of popular media, deeper investigation into the research that has been conducted in psychology and communication, as well as a few other fields, the analysis in sport grows. Evidence of the importance of peer relationships, team dynamics, as well as the growth of the sports as part of the global culture proves that further research and understanding of the interpersonal components of sport relationships is paramount.

Theory, in this instance communication theory, is utilized to help predict individual's behavior and explaining why that behavior takes place. Why is theory important to include in understanding these relationships? Because theory is *essential* to learning why past relationships have worked, or not worked, as well as what to improve upon, or continue when trying to facilitate successful relationships in the future. Whether it be the coach-athlete dynamic, the parent-child relationship, or even organizational and player connections to fans, success is the end goal. Theory allows individuals to break down experiences to parts, which then allows for a filtering of the good from the bad to help develop better communication practices the next time an interaction takes place. This text focuses on that breakdown and developmental growth in interactions.

Sport communication was built through an organizational theoretical base from the work of Nick Trujillo, and has grown beyond organizational perspectives to encompass the whole of what *sports* is. This look specifically at the interpersonal side sport is just one part, but an essential part of sports as the core of every team, every organization, and every league is relationship development. As stated above, this book looks in depth at the most important relationships in sports through examples from literature, television, movies, and historical texts to illustrate the connection to theory and the communication outcomes that are influenced.

This approach is in contrast to the case study method, which is the traditional method for connecting theory and practice in fields such as business, psychology, and communication. The biggest limitation of case studies, however, is the lack of nuance in the approach. Since case studies are either created de novo as examples, or are drawn from the experience of the authors, they are almost always new to the readers, and thus the only elements of the case that are available to readers are the ones that are explicitly stated by the authors. The value of this book's approach, then, is that, by drawing from our rich cultural store of shared "cases" from literature, television, movies, and history, all of the nuances and richness of character, context, and even nonverbal communication are instantly available to the reader to help them understand and analyze the case. Not only are the stories better, but the possibilities for analysis and discussion are exponentially increased. If a class is not familiar with one of this book's examples (or "cases"), the professor can easily share it with the class using YouTube or a similar resource, thus ensuring that everyone begins with the same base of knowledge. In the end, these richly textured examples are as close as we are likely to get in an introductory class to field research.

Finally, for professors of sport communication as users of this textbook, there are two additional advantages to this approach. First, the explicit focus on theory in sport communication interpersonal relationship development is unique and fills an important gap in sport communication textbooks. Second, as the professor becomes familiar and comfortable with the use of "cases" from popular culture and our shared cultural knowledge, he or she can easily begin to supplement the text with examples that are tailored to the experiences and knowledge of the class. As an author, I am always looking to grow my database of these types of "cases" as are many other professors, which is why I chose to write this book. I would encourage readers to share these with me as the field of knowledge always has room to grow.

I believe that this book is a uniquely enjoyable and useful application of theory to sport communication. I hope that you enjoy using it as much as I enjoyed writing it.

ABOUT THE AUTHOR

Dariela Rodriguez (Ph.D., University of Oklahoma, 2012) is an Associate Professor of Communication, and Coordinator of Sport Communication at Ashland University in Ashland, Ohio. Dr. Rodriguez' expertise is in interpersonal communication with a specialization in sport communication. She has published journal articles in publications such as *Communication Education, Qualitative Health Research,* and *Communication Research Reports.* Her current research includes work in concussion protocols and reporting in sport and leadership preferences of Millennial generation athletes.

CHAPTER 1

INTRODUCTION

Chapter Objectives

At the end of this chapter, readers will be able to:

1. Define sport.

2. List three uses of sport in human society.

3. Define communication.

4. Differentiate sport, play, work, and leisure.

5. Describe sports situations where autocratic, transformational, and transactional leadership styles would be appropriate.

Key Terms

Culture	Causal play	Transformational leadership
Sport	Communication	style
Leisure	Sport relationships	Transactional leadership style
Play	Coordinated management	Fandom
Work	of meaning	Fanship

Whether it be in American society or within societies throughout the world, sports and sport are a common language that can be spoken as part of human interaction and culture. Throughout the available recorded history of mankind, the presence of sporting events or activities have been associated with everything from war to religion to celebration to mourning. As societies expanded, so did sporting styles and practice. Just as sport has always been a part of our society, communication practices have spread in much the same way. The practice, style, meaning, and sharing of communication have expanded along with the growing structure of communication. The aim of this book is to spell out the theory and the practice of how communication works in an embedded style through sport.

HISTORY OF SPORT AND SOCIETY

Sport game-like activity requiring rules, containing a competitive element, and requiring a level of physical exertion.

"The treatment of **sport**, defined here as a game-like activity having rules, a competitive element, and requiring some form of physical exertion, has generally been included within the broader category 'games' in the history of anthropology" (Blanchard & Cheska, 1985, p. 14). Blanchard and Cheska (1985), in their book *The Anthropology of Sport: An Introduction*, outline the history of multiple civilizations through their practice of sport as a cultural building block. Sir Edward Burnett Tylor, usually referred to as the father of anthropology, was also one of the first to see sport as more of a window to the culture it exists in rather than just part of the cultural practices (1879, in Blanchard & Cheska, 1985). Though Tylor noted that some simple games may be incidental, others were clear indications of structure and practice that were unique to the culture itself.

SPORT AS A CULTURE

Culture the communication concepts of shared meaning and understanding within societies.

The concept of **culture** has always challenged researchers as to how to solidify a definition of this single word. When referring to fields such as sociology, anthropology, and communication, each field would try to define the term differently as it would be based on the *practice* of culture rather than the term itself. According to the definition in the Merriam-Webster Dictionary, culture is defined in multiple ways. First is "the beliefs, customs, arts, etc., of a particular society, group, place, or time" (www.merriam-webster.com). The second definition is, "a particular society that has its own beliefs, ways of life, art, etc." (www.merriam-webster.com). These two definitions can easily speak to what culture is and how it is utilized in the different fields of the social sciences; however, a combination of the two can create a suitable definition for a discussion of culture in sport and of sport's influence in culture.

When considering each of these definitions, commonalities include the attention to culture, art, and society practices. Beyond the definition of the word "culture" itself, what defines a culture can be (and has been) disputed by the different fields of social science for ages. For the purposes of this book, culture will not be defined by, but will include, the communication concepts of shared meaning and understanding within societies. One of those societies is the subculture of sport. To understand the concept and meaning of "sport," we first have to understand the differing concepts of work and leisure.

Leisure vs Work

According to Blanchard and Cheska (1985), the best way to understand "leisure" is to compare it to general understanding of work. We often associate **work** with purposeful activity where we see leisure as a lack of purposeful or structured activity. Taking the notion of leisure one step further, the idea of "play" is often closely associated with what we often consider leisure. It is not uncommon for people to call the weekend their leisure time, which is also usually filled with activities they consider fun, or play. Though **leisure** may be defined as "free time," this does not automatically equate to a complete lack of activity. It usually involves filling that time with activity we enjoy rather than *work* we are required to do.

> **Work** activity, usually requiring strength used towards completion of a need or duty.

> **Leisure** often considered free time, though usually time filled with activity

Billings, Butterworth, and Turman (2015), consider leisure as causal play. They differentiate this from sport by explaining that **causal play** is less organized and more rudimentary than sport which usually entails rules that are common across participation. For example, in the TV show *Friends*, there is an episode aptly titled "The One With The Ball" where Monica, Ross, Joey, and Chandler get caught up in a game where they are throwing around a Nerf-type ball for hours with the simple goal of not letting the ball fall or hit the ground (Bright, Crane, Kauffman, & Halverson, 1999). There is no purpose to the game, no rules beyond not letting the ball drop, and more likely than not there is not another team they would compete against on a regular basis in this game play scenario. To them, the game is crucial, to others, including Phoebe who ends up catching the ball and putting it down on the counter, the game is not even a game. This would be **play**.

> **Causal play** more rudimentary activity than sport as it usually entails rules that are common in participation in the particular game rather than a sport across a culture.

> **Play** associated with a game, activity towards recreational endeavors.

Sport vs Leisure

When play is given more work and more structure, then it becomes sport. Falling in line with structure comes detailed rules, often documented, as well as the chance for teams to play other teams in organized leagues and clubs, usually with even more specialized rules. These clubs include organizations such as the YMCA, the YWCA, the Amateur Athletic Union (AAU), and even Little League. The goal of these organizations is to create an opportunity for organized sport, which demand for has grown over the past several decades. Opportunities for youth

© Jacek_Kadaj/Shutterstock.com

sports, especially, are even expanding to leagues offered by neighborhood and church groups. The interest in competition is not new, but the outlet of organized sport consumption is increasingly becoming part of American (and the worldwide) culture, and it does not seem to be slowing down anytime soon. According to a study conducted by A.T. Kearney (2014), there was a 7 percent growth in the sports industry's worldwide gross domestic product (GDP) between 2009 and 2013. In 2009 the industry reported revenue of $58 billion dollars worldwide, which grew to $75 billion in 2013, and $80 billion in 2014. This represents larger growth than most countries have experienced in recent years, and is an indication that even in times of recession and financial stagnation, people are still willing to spend money on sports (www.atkearney.com, 2014).

Sport and Culture

Sport as a culture is no more evident than in the financial statistics listed above, but to fully understand just what individuals are spending their money on, the understanding of what sport means to a culture needs to be explained. When individuals play sports, it is often for fun, but what sports they play and why are usually part of a bigger cultural influence. Sports of all types have been played over the years of human existence. Games have been played

for political reasons, religious reasons, as well as fun. In 776 B.C., the Greeks founded the Olympic Games, of consisting of fewer "events" than the modern Olympics, but reflecting the sports that were both of interest and of use to the ancient Greek culture (Szymanski, 2009). The city-states that comprised the ancient Greek landscape were often involved in political conflict, including war, and each would usually hold its own sport festivals. The Olympics were a time for all the city-states to come together, compete, stop political and military conflict, and to honor Zeus.

The respect for peace during the Olympics is one tradition that changed along with the addition of events of the current Games. Though the athletes often stay away from the political battles of their countries, boycotts have been used as government protest of the politics of the host countries. With the battle between competitors often being comparable to the battles that take place in the fields of war (Blanchard & Cheska, 1985), it is no surprise that the sports and politics are often intertwined. In the aptly named mixed martial arts (MMA) film *Warrior*, the two main characters are set to fight in a MMA tournament (Sparta) to find out who is the world's toughest fighter. The fighters *battle* it out beginning each round with the referee calling for the fighters to "Go to war!" (O'Connor, O'Connor, & O'Connor, 2011).

For some factual examples, the *Miracle on Ice* hockey game in the 1980 Lake Placid Winter Olympics between the teams from the United States and the Soviet Union was seen by many as the only real battle of the Cold War. The success of African-American runner Jesse Owens in the 1936 Berlin Summer Olympics was seen as a political attack against the eugenic-based racism of Adolf Hitler and his Nazi party. We identify successful athletes with modern day superheroes, especially those who are able to bring their success beyond sport, mainly because we live beyond sport.

© PANIGALE/Shutterstock.com

CULTURE AND COMMUNICATION

Part of our ability to bring these metaphors and heroes into our everyday life is through communication. **Communication** allows individuals to create meaning through the coding and decoding of language and nonverbal symbols. Through shared understanding of language and symbols, individuals are able to create the meaning to actually communicate. Sports have a way of developing this understanding without the need for an actual sharing of a language. Rules and symbols can often take the place of common spoken word. From there, sport has the ability to transform the communication platform.

Communication allows individuals to create meaning through the coding and decoding of language and nonverbal symbols.

In 1914, Germany and England were involved in battles along the Western Front that were part of the many battles of World War I (history.com). Though these battles were long standing and bloody on both sides, one of the most significant sports stories to come out of that time was a cease-fire between the soldiers form both sides on Christmas Day. Though Pope Benedict XV had suggested a cease-fire for the troops to celebrate the season, no country had actually taken the action of claiming an official hiatus (history.com). Though the warring countries did not take the steps to make the truce official, the troops did take advantage of the holiday to cross into the neutral zone, share gifts with their enemy, and for some, to play a friendly game of soccer among the singing of Christmas carols. This became known as the Christmas Truce of 1914, and is one of the last noted examples of chivalry in warfare on a large and noticeable basis (history.com). The story of Nelson Mandela bringing the people of South Africa together around the success of the Springboks during the 1995 Rugby World Cup is another example of how sports have been able to have healing power even in the face of long standing political crisis (Clearly, 2013).

RELATIONSHIPS IN SPORT

Beyond the cultures and languages that sport can change, consumption of sport, through individual participation or even fandom, can impact relationships in many different ways. The concept of this text is to discuss just how this can take place from the standpoint of theoretical communication. Specifically, we will discuss how sports can influence the practice of interpersonal and relational communication. Each of the chapters investigates how different relationships exist in a sports setting as well as how the understanding and practice of behaviors involved in communication theory can predict and explain these relational dynamics.

Sport relationships
interpersonal relationships existing in and/or being influenced by the context of sport.

Sport relationships is defined here as interpersonal relationships existing in and/or being influenced by the context of sport. It may seem odd that the *context* of sport rather than the participation in sport is the influencing factor, but as explained earlier in the chapter, the culture of sport spreads beyond just participation. Focusing on the context within the definition allows for the examination and explanation of the multitude of relationships involved in sport. These include not only the more familiar and expected relationships between coaches and athletes and teammates, but they also include the broader scope of fandom, generational differences, as well as overarching group dynamics. Each of these relationships involves different interpersonal dynamics, but they also are governed by the communication that takes place in sport.

The Coach-Athlete Relationship

This relationship between a coach and their athlete is the core of most sport participation experiences. From the time children begin to play sports until the time a select few will retire as professional athletes, there is the opportunity for athletes to encounter countless leaders in the role of a "coach." This means that there are also countless opportunities for athletes to encounter many different types of coaches. Each and every time this relationship begins anew, each member of the relational dyad needs to build a new understanding of the communication that will define the progress of both the relational dynamic and the progress of the team as a whole.

Historic examples of intriguing coach-athlete relationships usually include the rebellious athlete and the overbearing coach. Usually the relationship is defined by anger, frustration, and resentment from both individuals. The issues

© Mitrofanov Alexander/Shutterstock.com

that exist at the core of the relationship are usually based on the lack of mutual understanding based on shared meaning and communication. What is most interesting, and also a catalyst for miscommunication, are the different contexts under which this relationship exists. Between practices, travel, meetings, and game settings, the communication between coaches and athletes can often range from more personal (during meetings and in travel settings) to more business/hierarchical in game and practice settings. With the differences in communication contexts allowing for often drastically different communication styles, the relational aspect of coach-athlete interactions can require more attention than many other relationships in sport.

Scholarship has identified two key aspects of relational communication as integral to success within the coach-athlete relationship: immediacy and efficacy. Although we give provisional definitions for these two terms here, they will be discussed in much greater detail and given more nuanced definitions in Chapter 2. For the purposes of this introduction, immediacy is the sense of liking that is experienced between two individuals. In non-sport based relationships, immediacy helps to move the relationship forward as the sense of liking for the communication partner builds a want to continue further communication between the two individuals. In a sport-based relationship, this sense of liking not only helps build the same bond as in the non-sport setting, but it also acts to help to balance out the more assertive communication that is required from a coach during the game and practice situations.

In the examples above, it is often the immediacy that keeps the more infamous coach-athlete relationships working towards success. Some of these include the University of Oregon's Bill Bowerman and Steve Prefontaine, the legendary track coach who created Nike running shoes and his star distance runner who could not help but to challenge Bowerman at nearly every turn. Bowerman insisted that his runners follow specific rules on and off the field, but "Pre," as he became known as, could not see why his technique or training regimen needed to be adapted. It was not until Pre realized that Bowerman was not against the young star or trying to trivialize his past success, but rather was trying to allow him to become even better than even Pre could imagine, that the two began to create a dynasty right inside Hayward Field. Though immediacy was an important factor in the building of this relationship, the second factor is that of efficacy.

Efficacy is a belief in one's ability to complete a task. In sports, often this is accompanied by both team and coaching efficacy. Efficacy is built through four factors listed by Bandura (1977; 1997): verbal persuasion, vicarious experiences, psychological states, and emotional arousal. Within the coach-athlete dynamic, verbal persuasion would take the form of positive feedback from the coach as to the athlete's performance. Though criticism is necessary to teach the skill needed in the sport, once that skill is mastered, the coach needs to make sure to include positive feedback to help develop the sense of efficacy. Of the four factors, verbal persuasion works hand in hand with the building of immediacy to help forge a stronger relationship between coaching and athletes.

Family Communication in Sport

When individuals decide to participate in a sport, often the individuals most affected by their participation aside from the athlete him or herself are the families. Specifically, when the athlete is young, the impact of sport participation will have a stronger impact on the relationships in the athlete's lives than when they enter into a relationship already participating in sports. The relationship

© bikeriderlondon/Shutterstock.com

at the heart of most sport based research focusing on family communication looks at youth-aged to young-adult aged athletes and their families. This research has described the changes in family dynamics generated by child's sport participation as well as the impact on the family communication styles, including content and context.

When a child begins to participate in a sport, there is usually one of two reasons for beginning to play; either the parent has selected the sport so the youngster can try it out, or the child him or herself has asked to play. If the parents have decided to register their child for a sport, often it is a sport in which the parent or parents have played in the past, one they understand, and one in which they believe their child will be successful while playing. This often means the parent has at least a basic knowledge of the sport, and therefore will be able to communicate about the sport with the child, including teaching the young athlete about the rules, play, and even history of the sport. The parent may not be overly concerned with the cost of equipment and the time needed to dedicate to the sport, as he or she is the one who selected the sport in the beginning. This often will result in positive communication between the child and parent about the sport, assuming that whether or not the child enjoys the sport does not raise issues between the two.

This previous scenario does not mean that disaster will be the outcome of a child selecting to participate in a sport that is unknown to their parents; things are never that black and white. It will, however, create a situation where the parent and the child will work together to develop a new type of communication dynamic when the conversations surround the context of the child's sport participation. For example, imagine a young man or woman in the United States who wants to play rugby. Now, this is not a completely foreign sport, but it is also one that is not as common as baseball or basketball in the United States. He or she will have opportunities to play; however, his or her parent may need to be educating himself or herself about this new sport just to have a conversation about practice. Rugby is not often on television in the United States, it is not played in every school or recreation center, and therefore is not as easy to access and therefore learn. Part of communicating for parents and children about sport entails learning how to communicate about a sport, from the rules of the game to support and motivation for their young athlete.

As is evident, communication within families concerning sports and sport participation can lead to both positive and negative outcomes depending on whether or not clear understanding is communicated between the parent and his or her athlete. If the athlete is enjoying his or her experience or not, if he or she is seeking to take their athletic training to the next level of competition, or even if they just want to know more about the sport, it is important that both parties are in full understanding of the meaning of both the communication taking place and the context of said communication. The **coordinated management of meaning** describes how individuals in a conversation can work to generate understanding in the communication process, which equates to coordination of intended and understood meaning between the two parties.

© bikeriderlondon/Shutterstock.com

Once meaning is understood, accommodating communication between the partners is essential to successful communication. If parents are not able to accommodate their communication to be able to show their support or generate motivational messages when needed, the athlete may not be able to generation meaning and understanding from the messages. Essentially, family communication in sports goes far beyond discussions about practice/game schedules and player statistics. Done well, it can mean a future in sports that can go beyond the high school or even college level. When it falls apart, it can end a great playing career before it has a chance to start.

Millennial Athletes

Communication between parents and athletes and/or the coach and his or her players is obviously a complicated process, as the above suggests, but lately communication practices between these groups have been further complicated by the unique issues associated with the Millennial Generation. Though communication in families and in sport has always had members of different generations as half of the dyad, and it is natural for the generations to change through the progression of time, never has a generation made as large of an impact on their society as has the Millennial Generation (Alsop, 2008; Huntley, 2006; Twenge, 2006).

The Millennial Generation, or Generation Y, are those individuals who were born between 1982 and 2002, and they have been changing the world ever since they came into it. This generation is truly the product of their environment, including helicopter parenting, growing up in a digital society, growing up during the war on terror, as well as consumer marketing realizing that they are one of the largest generations in several decades and learning to cater to the Millennials nearly since birth (Alsop, 2008; Huntley, 2006; Twenge, 2006). Many argue that this generation has grown up with a sense of entitlement shown most prevalently through the constant questions being asked by the young members of this generation which seem to challenge the authority of those in power positions. Teachers, principals, professors, university administrators, and members of corporate hierarchies have all identified this new generation's potential but also noted

Coordinated management of meaning how individuals in a conversation generate understanding in the communication process, which equates to coordination of intended and understood meaning between the two parties.

this questioning behavior as a drawback of engaging with members of Generation Y (Alsop, 2008; Huntley, 2006; Twenge, 2006). Though this behavior has been seen as a negative, it is also a communication behavior that may need a second look when it is put into a sport context.

In the past, the autocratic, loud, often aggressive communication that accompanies the relationship between coaches and athletes was the norm, as was mentioned before. However, this approach to coaching has been under fire throughout the years as many have found that athletes were not responding to this assertive approach. Athletes did not want someone who would just yell, but rather wanted someone who included them in the process, meaning they wanted to be part of the game decision-making rather than just being seen as someone who was simply expected to follow orders. The interaction between the Millennials and their coaches is one that is still under investigation, as communication and sport psychology researchers are trying to determine the exact level of impact that this new generation is having on the sport environment. From the coaching example above, to the process of recruiting in the collegiate ranks, to the increase in transfers because of freshmen not playing during their first year, to student athletes being critical as well as criticized on social media are all factors that point to Millennial influence in sport communication.

Group Communication

Being an athlete is often a solitary effort. Motivating oneself to work hard, to go to practice, to watch film and look over playbooks is all based on self-discipline and an interest in bettering oneself. The difference between athletes in solo sports such as tennis or even individual events in track and field, and those in team sports such as basketball and hockey, is that this motivation to devote a substantial amount of time to a team is often generated by a commitment to the team as well as the sport. This story has been seen played out time and time again in sport, as well as by Hollywood. Movies such as *Remember the Titans*, *When the Game Stands Tall*, and *Miracle* are all more about the value and meaning of the word "team" than they are about the overall accomplishment of the team. Though the movie of the Miracle on Ice would not have been made if the Team USA hockey players did not beat the Soviet team and win Olympic gold, the game itself was only part of the movie. Seeing how the team came together by generating a sense of cohesion was what made the film interesting and worth the price of admission, so to speak.

What makes good teams great, or even teams successful in general, is a sense of cohesion between members of the team. Cohesion in sports can be defined as the ability of a team to work as a unit towards a common goal. In sport this goal can be based on a successful season, a win in a rivalry game, or even dedicating a season to specific person. It is cohesion that allows players to hold each other accountable for the work needed to be successful throughout the season. Cohesion can be built in many different ways. From working together in practice, to traveling together to games, to working through the pressures of success and/or failure, all of these factors, and so many more, can bring a team together. While fans appreciate what true teamwork looks like, it is very obvious what a team that is lacking in cohesion looks like.

For years the Los Angeles Lakers were the team to beat, or the team to get traded to if you were an NBA player. From the teams with Kareem Abdul-Jabbar and Magic Johnson winning multiple championships in the 1980's to those with Kobe Bryant, Shaquille O'Neal, and Derek Fisher in the 2000's, the purple and gold were the gold standard when it came to teamwork. They brought some of the best individual players in the game to the franchise and turned them into a team. This is not easy, as egos can often get in the way at the professional level, but the Lakers were able to do it and do it well. Fast-forward to the present and the Lakers are just trying to pull players together who are willing to play together. The team has been struggling with internal issues working with their former star, Kobe Bryant. As more and more players are vocal about not wanting to play with Bryant (Helin, 2015), it is impacting the cohesion on the team and therefore the team success. If you juxtapose this with the ability of teams such as the San Antonio Spurs to mix old and young players, team veteran with players new to the organization, and players from multiple different countries and cultures, the concept of how to create a thriving and fluid sense of teamwork through cohesion is on display every game.

Leadership

Coaches, team captains, the unsung hero of the team; one thing all these individuals have in common is leadership ability that their teammates look to as a means to guide the team through practices, games, and seasons. Being a leader is not about being in charge as much as it is about an individual who is able to guide others in a specific direction. It can be said that the mark of a leader is often the ability to persuade others to follow your ideas or your plan. Having said this, the mark of a good leader could be identified as one who not only leads, but also participates in the process he or she is asking his or her subordinates to undertake. This is especially important in sport leadership.

When considering the leadership styles of coaches, as was stated before, the typical autocratic and democratic leadership styles are often those that come to mind. Though these two styles are easy to identify, those in the field of leadership research have been able to identify other leader behaviors that have translated into other styles. For example, transactional and transformational leaders are becoming more and more prevalent in both the corporate world and the world of sports. These leaders have been defined as residing in between autocratic, democratic, and laissez-faire leaders on the spectrum. Specifically,

© turgaygundogdu/Shutterstock.com

Transformational leadership style a leadership style that would be placed between the aggressive style of the autocratic leader and the more participative leadership style of the democratic leader.

Transactional leadership style a leadership style where the leader shares a substantial amount of power with their group members and tends to focus on the end result rather than process.

transformational leaders would be placed between the aggressive style of the autocratic leader and the more participative leadership style of the democratic leader (Bass, 1985; Bass, Avolio, & Atwater, 1996). These leaders are seen as more willing to give decision-making power to their subordinates, but are able to keep a strong enough presence as a leader to take control when they deem necessary. An example of this would be a professional coach who can give play-calling duties to his or her star athlete based on the preset game plan. The coaching staff has set the parameters of the team's approach to the game which is to be followed; however, the player is able to execute that plan as he or she sees necessary.

A **transactional leader** tends to be more liberal in the distribution of power than autocratic, transformational, or democratic leaders. Sitting in between democratic and laissez-faire leaders, transactional leaders share a substantial amount of power with their group members and tend to focus on the end result being completed successfully rather than the process of how to get there (Bass et al., 1996). Because of their tendency towards the laissez-faire type of management where they assess the nature of the group when the task has failed or succeeded, this type of leader often misses problems until they are possible hindrances to the group's task or goal. Transactional leaders can succeed if all of the members of their group are self motivated; however, often the lack of success within these groups is caused by the perceived lack of importance of the task and lack of appreciation from the leader for their work that is commonly felt by the group members.

These types of leaders are often researched from the perspective of the coach towards the athlete; however, discounting the leadership from teammate to teammate results in missing the alternative leadership outlets available and utilized in sports. Individuals such as team captains, team spiritual leaders, and those who provide leadership while coming off of the bench (e.g., basketball's 6th man) are all often-utilized yet sometimes-unrecognized members of the leadership team in sports. One of the best-known 6th man role players in the NBA at the current moment is Manu Ginóbili from the San Antonio Spurs. Though his influence comes off of the bench for the Spurs, he has been a team captain and starter for the Argentinian National Team during world tournament play, including the Olympics. Though each of these roles requires different leadership styles, Ginóbili has always been able to step into the role required and requested of him depending on the needs of the team. Though many will say that leadership comes from a specific personality, the current research shows that circumstance also plays a large role in who steps in as a group leader as well as the style of leadership they practice. Great leaders allow their situation to determine the styles rather than trying to utilize a one-size-fits-all mentality for all their different roles.

For example, a basketball coach may find his or her team to be undisciplined at the beginning of the season and may need more of an autocratic approach while learning practice schedules and drills as well as plays and game situations. As the team learns what is expected of them, the coach may let the captains run warm-up drills and the stretching session at the beginning of the practices. As the season progresses, the coach could allow the team to make suggestions during timeouts and quarter breaks depending on what they are seeing or experiencing on the court. Some suggestions may be implemented, and some may not depending on the coach's analysis of the team and the opponent; however, allowing suggestions to be made is a move towards shared responsibility. This is a prime example of a good leader matching skills to circumstances. Often this scenario will develop through the burgeoning of team leaders among the player ranks because of sharing of power and decision-making abilities.

Fandom

Another aspect of interpersonal communication that again can lead to group communication is the association of an individual with a team as a fan. **Fandom**, as it is commonly referred to in both mainstream media and social scientific research, is the connection that one individual has with another when each are fans of a particular sport team or athlete (Reysen & Branscombe, 2010). Where **fanship** describes one's connection to a particular team or individual athlete, fandom is the connection to other likeminded fans. Fandom has the ability to bring family and friends, but also complete strangers, together. It is not uncommon to see alumni groups getting together to support their alma mater's athletic teams in cities around the globe. The only thing that many of the individuals in these groups have in common upon meeting for the first time is the connection to their university and its teams. However, this often is all these fans need to start off a conversation . . . that and a little fanship. Once they are able to get to know more about each other, fandom grows to friendship and perhaps meetings outside of the alumni group settings.

Fandom the connection that one individual has with another when each are fans of a particular sport team or athlete.

Fanship one's connection to a particular team or individual athlete.

Often the growth of fanship, and therefore the development of fandom, stems from the influence of family or friends at a young age. For example, if your family are New York Jets fans and all you see on TV and hear about as a child growing up are stories of the New York Jets, you could be living in California all of your life yet be a fan of the Jets. The same can be said for connections made with friends, especially later in life. Assume the same scenario of you growing up in sunny California, but now we will talk a little basketball. Though the Warriors took some time to get started, you always believed in the greatness of the team and the potential of the 2015

© Corepics VOF/Shutterstock.com

NBA Championship. Though you are still a Warriors fan, you are also a fan of basketball and love going to see games live. Upon moving to Chicago for your new job, you miss the live game environment and miss seeing games with your friends, but all of your new friends are Chicago Bulls fans. As time goes by, you start to watch more Bulls games on TV, start going out with your friends to catch games after work, and eventually catch some live games. The connection of fandom leads you to become a Bulls fan . . . as your second favorite team, of course. This shows how location can influence fanship and fandom.

CONCLUSION

This book defines the intricate connection between sports and communication. Each chapter will bring together communication theory and different interpersonal relationships that help define the landscape of relational communication in sport. With the growth of sport communication, there is a need to help define the many different divisions that make up the field. The influence of interpersonal relationships resonates through all aspects of sports, as identified above. An understanding of the explanatory and predictive power of theory can only help make these relationships stronger. As stated at the beginning of the chapter, sports have been part of developing societies since the beginning of recorded history. Often Aztec and Mayan tribes set up their sports arenas before any other structures when they moved from one location to another. The importance of sports in developing culture and communication cannot be overstated, and will be defined and discussed in detail in the rest of this book.

DISCUSSION QUESTIONS

1. Does the structure of play enhance or diminish the enjoyment of sports?
2. Though culture has helped cultivate the growth of sport, how does culture currently influence the sports that individuals play? Consider region, age, gender, etc.
3. The influence of communication in everyday life is understood as crucial to our existence. How can communication be utilized in sports with the same effect in sports?

REFERENCES

Alsop, R. (2008). *The trophy kids grow up: How the millennial generation is shaking up the workplace.* San Francisco, CA: Jossey-Bass.

A.T. Kearney study: Sports industry growing faster than GDP (2014). Retrieved from https://www.atkearney.com/news-media/news-releases/news-release/-/asset_publisher/00OIL7Jc67KL/content/id/5273085.

Bandura, A. (1977). Self-efficacy: Towards a unifying theory of behavioral change. *Psychological Review, 84,* 191-215. http://dx.doi.org/10.1037/0033-295X.84.2.191

Bandura, A. (1997). *Self-efficacy: The exercise of control.* New York: Freeman.

Bass, B.M. (1985). *Leadership and performance beyond expectations.* New York: The Free Press.

Bass, B.M., Avolio, B.J., & Atwater, L. (1996). The transformational and transactional leadership of men and women. *Applied Psychology: An International Review, 45(1),* 5–34.

Billings, A.C., Butterworth, M.L., & Turman, P.D. (2015). *Communication and Sport.* Thousand Oaks, CA: SAGE Publications, Inc.

Bright, K. (Producer), Crane, D. (Producer), Kauffman, M. (Producer), Halverson, G (Director). (1999). The one with the ball [Television series episode]. In A. Richard [Producer], *Friends.* Burbank, CA: Warner Brothers.

Blanchard, K., & Cheska, A. (1985). *The anthropology of sport: An introduction.* South Hadley. MA: Bergin & Garvey Publishers.

Helin, K. (2015). Bucks' Jared Dudley: "Most guys don't want to play with Kobe". *NBC Sports.* Retrieved from http://nba.nbcsports.com/2015/05/27/bucks-jared-dudley-most-guys-dont-want-to-play-with-kobe/.

Huntley, R. (2006). *The world according to y: Inside the new adult generation.* Crows Nest, NSW: Allen & Unwin.

O'Connor, G. (Producer), O'Connor, G (Producer), O'Connor, G. (Director). (2011). *Warrior* [Motion Picture]. USA: Lionsgate.

Reysen, S., & Branscombe, N.R. (2010). Fanship and fandom: Comparisons between sport and non-sport fans. *Journal of Sport Behavior, 33(2),* 176–193.

Szymanski, S. (2009). *Playbooks and checkbooks: An introduction to the economics of modern sports.* Princeton, NJ: Princeton University Press.

Twenge, J.M. (2006). *Generation me: Why today's young Americans are more confident, assertive, entitled – and more miserable then ever before.* New York: Free Press.

Tylor, E.B. (1871). *Primitive culture: Researches into the development of — mythology, philosophy, religion, language, art, and custom.* London: J. Murray.

CHAPTER 2

THE COACH-ATHLETE RELATIONSHIP

Chapter Objectives

At the end of this chapter, readers will be able to:

1. Describe how coaches can use immediacy to build the efficacy of their athletes.

2. Explain why coaches need to balance immediacy and feedback in their coaching.

3. List three nonverbal immediacy behaviors and three nonverbal immediacy behaviors.

4. Give an example of times when they have used anticipatory regret messaging.

Key Terms

Immediacy	Verbal persuasion	Regret messaging
Efficacy	Vicarious experience	(counterfactual and
Self-efficacy	Live modeling	anticipatory)
Team efficacy	Symbolic modeling	

INTRODUCTION

It is a blistering hot summer day in the fictional town of Dillon, Texas, home of the fabled Dillon Panthers in the acclaimed television show, *Friday Night Lights*. In the series pilot episode, viewers are introduced to the Panthers football players and see that the eyes of an entire city are on the Panthers to bring home a state championship. It is the first day of summer two-a-days and new head coach Eric Taylor and his staff are busy getting their football team ready for the new season. We see the typical swagger of teenage boys who are considered kings in their small town, but by the end of that first episode, we see that the team has suffered a major setback with the loss of quarterback Jason Street to injury (Berg, Aubrey, Freed, & Cameron, 2011). Though one of his star players is out for the season, this does not reduce the pressure on Coach Taylor and the Panthers to win state—the only thing that matters in the state of Texas from August to December. This fictional depiction of life, and the pressures of sport, in small town Texas focuses not only on the relationships between the players and their peers in Dillon High School, but goes in depth into the relationships that Coach Taylor forms with many of his athletes. We see the importance of creating a sense of immediacy with each individual athlete, as well as each athlete as an individual. Viewers also see how the immediate relationships help create a sense of efficacy within the athlete, allowing the most unassuming of heroes to surface throughout the progression of the show. This chapter will look at the theories of immediacy and efficacy and how each relates to the success of coaches and their athletes.

© Michael Langish/Shutterstock.com

The relationship between a coach and his or her team is often a balancing act among discipline, power, appreciation, and education. This balancing act can often be made easier through the use of immediacy within the relationship. Creating a sense of efficacy, or a sense of one's ability, in athletes is often a difficult task as well, considering most of what a coach says during practice and/or game situations revolves around discipline or correction of a player's behaviors and efforts (Vargas-Tonsing, Meyers, & Feltz, 2004). This is often when the balance between immediacy and feedback come into play to build athlete efficacy (Vargas-Tonsing, Meyers, & Feltz, 2004).

IMMEDIACY AND EFFICACY DEFINED

The first issues to be addressed are: what is immediacy and what exactly is efficacy? Immediacy in the field of communication studies has been defined as an individual's ability to demonstrate that they are open for communication through both verbal and nonverbal means (Rubin & Martin, 1994). In the field of sport research, **immediacy** has been defined as the comfort and/or closeness that are perceived to be shared between the players and the coaches on a team (Rocca, Martin, & Toale, 1998). Examples of a strong immediate relationship between a coach and his or her athletes can be seen in the celebratory, or consoling, hugs coaches give to athletes when they walk off the playing field. Consider a professional athlete and his or her coach as an employee and boss. How often does a boss hug their employee after a bad day? The unique relationship that exists between coaches and athletes allows for many behaviors to take place that would usually not happen in other interpersonal or group settings. This concept will be explored further throughout the chapter.

Immediacy the comfort and/or closeness that are perceived to be shared between the players and the coaches on a team.

© Eugene Onischenko/Shutterstock.com

SELF-EFFICACY

According to Bandura (1977), an individual's sense of **self-efficacy** is based on one's perception of their own performance during, as well as in the final outcome, of a task. Four sources of self-efficacy are performance accomplishments, vicarious experiences, verbal persuasion, and/or emotional arousal (Bandura, 1977). In sports, a positive or negative sense of self-efficacy is usually based on whether an athlete is satisfied with the outcome of a performance. A positive sense of self-efficacy is usually the basis for continuing to build on success, leading to further goal-setting behavior and future achievements based on the outcome of the goal-seeking behavior (Burke, Peterson & Nix, 1995; Rocca et al., 1998; Richmond & McCroskey, 2000). How a coach's behavior can influence an athlete's efficacy will also be detailed further.

Self-efficacy one's perception of their own performance during, as well as in the final outcome, of a task.

THE IMMEDIATE RELATIONSHIP

From Pop Warner Football to the NFL, no matter the context of the dyad within the relationship, the communication between a coach and an athlete will always will be multifaceted and complicated. The reason for the difficulty within the coach-athlete dynamic resides in the fact that this relationship does not only exist in the realm of sports, but also has a strong interpersonal component, as well. Coaches often have to use assertive communication on the field during games and practices, which results in the need for immediacy to counter balance the behavior (Amorose & Weiss, 1998; Matsui, Kakuyama, & Onglatco, 1987; Rocca et al., 1998). The need for immediacy in these relationships often resides in the lack of power balance between the individuals involved, much like those between teachers and students in the classroom (Rocca et al., 1998; Turman & Schrodt, 2004).

As stated before, immediacy in the field of sports is the perceived comfort and/or closeness that is shared between a coach and his or her athletes (Rocca et al., 1998). Research has often compared this to the teacher-student relationship because of the education factor that is an essential component to the coach-athlete relationship (Rocca et al., 1998; Turman & Schrodt, 2004).

The difference between the teacher-student relationship and that of the coach and athlete dynamic is the amount of time coaches spend with their teams both on and off the field. For example, a high school teacher will spend class time with his or her students as part of the everyday routine of school; however, once the class ends, the students often will move to their next class and interact with a new teacher. The time spent between the teacher and the student is limited to the structure of the school day, assuming that the teacher does not have to meet with the student about grades or behavior issues before or after class. The coach also has set times for practices and games that structure the standard time they will have to spend with their athletes; however, once practice or games are over, the time spent interacting with the athlete is often not over.

© Tooties/Shutterstock.com

Keeping with the example of the high school student-athletes, when you look at the practice and game schedule of a sports team, the times listed on any formal schedule are actually just a fraction of the time a coach spends with the team. There can be team meetings before and after the practices and games, travel to and from the events, tournaments (depending on the sport) when teams spend a lot of non-playing time together between games, etc. When teams spend an abundance of time together it is easy for the relationships between coaches and athletes to become more familiar and create a sense of family (Rocca et al., 1998; Turman & Schrodt, 2004). As coaches work to maneuver the difficult job of leading a team, it is important for everyone to realize how to keep a sense of comfort within the team while still keeping the coach's sense of leadership and power intact.

LIFE BEFORE FRIDAY NIGHT

Taking a look back at the example from the show *Friday Night Lights*, when we first see the Dillon Panthers and Coach Taylor, the mood is anything but light. In the opening scenes of the show, Coach Taylor looks like a stereotypical coach, screaming at his players, making them run, tackle, run some more, calling out plays and yelling in faces of players who do not execute correctly. This is in stark contrast to the next scene when Coach is being interviewed and is seen praising Jason Street for his talent, skill, and work ethic. Though these scenes show two different sides of Coach Taylor, they also demonstrate two of the many different dynamics that are present between coaches and athletes. If the coach did not praise his football players as much as he yelled at them, it could jeopardize the performance of the team due to the lack of immediacy. The immediate relationship is necessary to establish a sense of trust, both in the techniques that a coach uses to lead as well as the overarching philosophy around which the team is centered (Rocca et al., 1998; Turman and Schrodt, 2004).

Albert Mehrabian's work on immediacy was a catalyst for more current work in communication-based immediacy research, namely the work of Virginia Richmond and her colleagues who established the "principle of immediate communication" (Richmond, McCroskey, & Johnson, 2003). Though research on immediacy has taken place in much of the social sciences, the use of communication to help establish the immediate interpersonal relationships is the format that is most important in sport communication. Starting with Mehrabian (1972), the *immediacy principle* initially stated that individuals will be/are interested in, or drawn to, those things that they find alluring, and logically will avoid those things that they do not appreciate. Applying this to sports, the principle would conclude that an athlete would want to continue playing a sport that he/she is enjoying playing, and not continue one that is not enjoyable. This clearly does not seem like a moment of sudden epiphany, as individuals tend to experience this nearly every day. For example, if someone does not like a particular food, he or she does not eat it. If we do not like a particular sports team, we do not cheer for them. However, taking this concept of acceptance and avoidance and transferring the behaviors to human interaction helps to explain how and why individuals interact and communicate with each individual they encounter as an *individual* (Mehrabian, 1972; Richmond & McCroskey, 2000; Richmond et al., 2000). In sports, the immediacy principle can help to explain why coaches interact differently with each player on a team, and why trying to treat each player the same can actually hurt the team more than it can help.

Moving the work of Mehrabian (1972) to a communication perspective, Virginia Richmond and colleagues (2003) established the *principle of immediate communication* as a means to help explain how immediacy influences day-to-day interactions. Immediacy behaviors in communication are rarely as simple as attraction or avoidance, but rather encompass many different verbal and nonverbal behaviors that are used to create the perception of immediacy or a lack thereof (Richmond et al., 2003). Immediate behaviors can, and usually do, vary depending on the intent of the communication encounter, as well as the individuals who are participating in the conversation (Richmond et al., 2003). An example of how these verbal and nonverbal behaviors are contextual in nature can be seen in the differences between how coaches and teachers interact with their athletes/students. In the classroom, praise for a student will usually take the form of verbal praise (e.g., "way to go", or "good job") along with nonverbal cues such as a smile. Though the verbal praise from a coach may take the same form as a teacher's verbally, the nonverbal praise is often different.

© Laura Stone/Shutterstock.com

Coaches can be seen jumping up and down on the sideline, pumping their fists after a play, or giving the hug mentioned in the beginning of the chapter; however, teachers would not generally perform these behaviors in a classroom. Immediacy in communication is clearly contextual (Richmond et al., 2003), and as such, the creation of an immediate relationship needs to be addressed in a very deliberate manner.

In general, **nonverbal immediacy behaviors** can include behaviors such as non-threatening touches (e.g., the high fives or pats on the back), smiling or eye contact during conversation (as mentioned in teacher-student relationships), or even animated speaking (e.g., an enthusiastic pre-game speech) (Richmond et al., 2003). These may seem like basic tools that any individual would use in everyday conversation, and the truth is they are. However, when used intentionally, nonverbal and verbal immediacy skills can be used to help create positive interpersonal relationships in a multitude of situations (Richmond et al., 2000).

The messages that coaches send to each of their athletes often vary greatly from moment to moment. A coach can correct a player's behavior, then discipline counterproductive behavior, and follow up with words of encouragement, all within the span of one game or one practice. Coaches often play the role of leader, motivator, teacher, mentor, confidant, parent, and friend (Haselwood, Joyner, Burke, Geyerman, Czech, Munkasy, & Zwald, 2005; Pogue & AhYun, 2006). The messages they send have to convey each of these roles, often simultaneously (Pouge & An Yun, 2006). Messages of encouragement can easily be used to help build immediacy as they are positive and convey what the individual is doing correctly. As much as positive feedback would make building immediacy easy, the need for performance feedback is part of sports, and this feedback includes negative feedback by way of corrective messages.

Negative feedback needs to be balanced or the athlete will not be able to see past the coach telling them what they do wrong in order to fix the problem (Black & Weiss, 1992). The messages can also act as a counter to the positive relationship that the coach should be attempting to create (Amorose & Weiss, 1998). A coach needs to understand how to give feedback in a manner that will allow the athlete to know that he or she is doing something wrong, or that they need to work harder, without running the risk of negative affect on behalf of the athlete (Amorose & Weiss, 1998). An established immediate relationship can help avoid a negative situation (Amorose & Weiss, 1998). Creating a sense of immediacy through the use of positive feedback within the coach-athlete relationship will allow the coach to be the leader they need to be while still creating a situation where the athlete is comfortable seeking further guidance, or feedback, from his or her coach (Amorose & Weiss, 1998). Negative feedback is not necessarily negative communication, but more criticism of the athlete's performance, which could be damaging sans the immediacy within the coach-athlete dyad (Amorose & Weiss, 1998).

Though the negative feedback is often critical in that it is meant to correct athlete behavior, it is also part of establishing an immediate relationship if the athlete understands that the messages are intended to help them, thereby

Nonverbal immediacy behaviors can include behaviors such as non-threatening touches, smiling or eye contact during conversation, or even animated speaking.

creating the perception that the coach wants the athlete to succeed and therefore is giving the corrective messages to help the athlete and not hurt him or her (Amorose & Weiss, 1998). When giving negative feedback, the nonverbal messages are important for helping the athlete understand that the coach is, in fact, looking out for the athlete's best interests (Black & Weiss, 1992). If the nonverbal communication of the coach is too aggressive while delivering corrective messages, the immediacy can be lost and lead to a negative reaction from the athlete (Black & Weiss, 1992). This is where the behaviors such as a hand on an athlete's shoulder, a calm tone of voice, or eye contact can perpetuate the perception of immediacy within the conversation. The immediate behavior can also create a sense of motivation on the part of the athlete to make the suggested corrections and increase his or her perceived competence level (Black & Weiss, 1992). This in turn can help with the next aspect of the coach-athlete relationship, which is efficacy.

IMMEDIACY AND ATHLETE PERFORMANCES

Traveling back to Dillon, Texas for a moment, we arrive on a Thursday night before one of many "big games" the team always seems to prepare for. After quarterback Jason Street goes down in the first game of the season, the inexperienced Matt Searson is looked towards to lead the Panthers on their drive towards the state championship. Where Street had talent, experience, and confidence, Searson has doubt, fear, and is extremely shy and soft spoken. Not exactly traits that would help him lead one of the top football teams in the state. Where Street knew Coach Taylor from his time playing youth football, Searson only knew Coach as his new coach, essentially establishing a lack of immediacy. Understanding the need for a quarterback to know his coach trusts him, and the efficacy that can come from this trust, Coach seeks Matt out the night before the game to let the young man know that he understands his fear and frustration, but that he has faith in him to lead the team. In the scene, Coach Taylor tells Matt that he understands the pressures that have been thrust upon him, but that his team believes in him as do his coaches. He lets him know he is proud of Matt for handling the situation so well and that on Friday night, he trusts Matt can be successful if the young man can trust himself.

Trust between a coach and his or her athlete is crucial to creating a positive team environment. If coaches want their athletes to keep playing and improving, it is important that the coaches are able to establish a trust in the athlete's skills through the trust that the feedback that they are giving, and the manner in which they are giving it, are in the best interest of the athletes on the team (Chelladurai,

© Pete Saloutos/Shutterstock.com

1984; Kassing & Infante, 1999; Rocca et al., 1998; Turman, 2003; Turman, 2005 Westre & Weiss, 1991).

SELF-EFFICACY IN SPORT

In his original work on self-efficacy, Bandura (1977) defined **self-efficacy** as a performance-based outcome that influences an individual's sense of ability or skill. In sports, self-efficacy will usually influence an athlete's choice of sport participation, the level of effort they expend, the level of persistence, and the level of attained achievement (Weigand & Stockman, 2000). Sport-based self-efficacy is often measured by examining the number of tasks players are expected to successfully complete as part of a specific task, whether or not an athlete has assurances that he or she will succeed in executing the task assigned, and the number of skills or sport areas an athlete in which perceives that he or she is knowledgeably skilled (Weigand & Stockman, 2000). Athletes can develop this sense on their own; however, in a team sport setting, coaches and teammates are crucial to the development of perceived efficacy. The influence of coaches and fellow teammates is only as strong as the trust that an athlete has with these individuals. Because trust is created through the development of an immediate relationship, it can be argued that the concepts of immediacy and self-efficacy are intricately linked.

BRINGING IT TOGETHER

Team efficacy the belief that a team has the skill to complete a given task together.

Verbal persuasion positive informational feedback.

Beyond immediacy, an individual's self-efficacy is influenced by accomplishments based on individual performance, messages based on verbal persuasion, vicarious experiences, psychological states, as well as emotional arousal (Bandura 1977; 1997). Though all factors have strong influences on one's sense of efficacy, in athletics, verbal persuasion has been forced to be one of the primary methods available to coaches to help build self-efficacy, as well as **team efficacy** among their fellow athletes (Vargas-Tonsing et al., 2004). **Verbal persuasion**, or positive informational feedback (Bandura, 1977; 1997), has been found to benefit athletic performance as it increases an athlete's perception of his or her own skill level, as well as the perception of the ability of his or her team (Vargas-Tonsing & Bartholemew, 2006). The perceived higher skill level, influenced through verbal persuasion, usually translates to better performance outcomes, thereby increasing individual and team success (Vargas-Tonsing & Bartholemew, 2006). In a study comparing the effects of strategy-based pre-game speeches to emotion-based speeches, or verbally persuasive speeches, Vargas-Tonsing & Bartholemew (2006) found the latter to be more effective for creating higher levels of athlete reported self-efficacy prior to an imagined sporting event. Though emotion can be an effective motivator, the information given via the feedback at the root of verbal persuasion helped athletes understand the focus of the game scenario, and their role in it, thereby increasing self-efficacy.

Performance accomplishments are connected to the sense of accomplishment, or lack thereof, as a result of one either achieving or not achieving the desired result of a set goal (Feltz & Lirgg, 1998). For example, if an individual seeks to accomplish three tasks before the end of the day, and all three tasks are completed in the allotted time, this individual will have a higher sense of efficacy than the individual who is unable to complete all three tasks. In sports, setting team goals, and helping athletes regulate their own goal setting, is an important aspect of a coach's duties. As the leader of the team, the coach needs to understand that one particular team is not capable of achieving at the same level of another; each team is unique and team goals need to be set accordingly. Not recognizing this coaching need can cause problems for achieving team success, as continuously not achieving team goals can damage the potential for building self and team efficacy (Feltz & Lirgg, 1998).

Vicarious experiences can be defined as a process of modeling of experiences to benefit, and perhaps motivate, individuals' future behaviors (Bandura, 1977; 1997). Coaches are often able to provide these experiences for athletes by showing them film of a big game or championship celebration to give them a goal to work to complete. In the Disney movie *Miracle*, Coach Herb Brooks showed his team videos of the Soviet National Team scoring multiple goals and beating the National Hockey League All-Star team prior to the USA-USSR pre-Olympic match-up. Though it is not uncommon for a team to watch films of the opponent to learn the other team's tendencies, this film session was also used to show the members of Team USA exactly what they were facing in the fast-paced, high-powered offense of the Soviet National Team. This team played with a speed and precision that the USA would not have experienced previously, and the concern for Brooks was that, if the first time they saw the Soviet offense was in a game situation, the team efficacy would drop substantially as a result of the lack of preparation and expectations that the team would experience (Calio, 1980). The 1980 Winter Olympics in Lake Placid was being was being billed as a political showdown as much as an athletic showdown, and Brooks needed every technique available to make sure his team was ready to take the ice. Vicarious experiences can work as a motivator to attain a specific goal or to avoid a specific outcome; in this situation Brooks wanted his team to do both.

Two forms of modeling include live modeling and symbolic modeling. **Live modeling** involves an individual providing an example of what he or she is seeking from others. So in sports, a coach may show videos of how plays are executed correctly, or take a lesser skilled team to watch a higher skilled team play. For example, taking a freshman basketball team to watch a top-ranked varsity team play to see how the game "looks" when a team plays at a higher level and is able to work together. It is not uncommon to see youth teams at high school tournaments

Vicarious experience a process of modeling of experiences to benefit, and perhaps motivate, individuals' future behaviors.

Live modeling involves an individual providing an example of what he or she is seeking from others.

© mooinblack/Shutterstock.com

or championship games as a means for a coach to get his team excited about playing and pushing towards the future. High school sports, cheerleading, and dance teams often host clinics during their playing/performance season as a means to gather interest in the team for future students. These are usually during the season, usually the same day the team will perform, so the children who attend the clinic are able to watch the team in action after the clinic. For the youth teams who attend, this is a means of live modeling during the clinic and live performance.

Symbolic modeling requires individuals to use motivational methods such as visualization to help them achieve the tasks they have before them (Bandura, 1977, 1997). Coaches will sometimes require players to have a mental walk through where visualization is the focus of the practice session. Fighters often use shadow boxing as a way to warm up and to visualize a fight before they walk out to the ring. Other symbolic modeling methods such as regret messages have been used in sports to help motivate positive team performances. **Regret messages** are messages that express the possibility of an athlete feeling regret due to performing or not performing specific behaviors (Turman, 2005). There are two types of regret messages, counterfactual and anticipatory, that can be used in pre-game, half-time, or post-game speeches (Turman, 2005). **Counterfactual regret messages** are those that look to invoke regret about past experiences (Turman, 2005). For example, if a team is playing in the finals of the state playoffs, and had lost the game the year before, the coach could remind the team about how it felt to lose the year before, and remind them of what they need to do different to not feel those negative emotions again. Essentially, not to feel the same regret as they did the year before. **Anticipatory regret messages** express the possibility of regret about future actions (Turman, 2005). For example, messages that speak of the "next 48 minutes for the next 48 years of your life" are considered anticipatory regret messages.

The final aspect of self-efficacy is **emotional arousal**, which is interested in explaining how emotions such as excitement, fear, or nervousness can influence the behavior of individuals during certain events (Bandura, 1977; 1997). In sports, control of an athlete's emotional arousal is usually the focus of a coach's pre-game routine from warm-ups to speeches. When coaching the Florida Gators to multiple BCS National Championship wins, Urban Meyer had the team engage in the same pre-game routine that started the evening before every home and away game. This routine started the night before the game in the team hotel where the players and coaches attended a meeting, then dinner, more meetings, then more food (Martin, 2008). The purpose of this routine was to make sure that the players were focusing on the team from Friday night until after the game was finished on Saturday. This helped steady the emotions, either based on excitement or nerves, of players regardless of the opponent or possible impact of the game. Coach Meyer knew that every opponent was a threat no matter what their rank, conference, or experience level. He wanted his team to play every game with the same intensity as the one before or the one after, so keeping a routine allowed for the focus to stay the same no matter what the name was on the other team's jersey (Martin, 2008). Because emotions can influence the athlete's

Symbolic modeling using motivational methods such as visualization to help them achieve the tasks they have before them.

Counterfactual Regret motivational messages that that look to invoke regret about past experiences.

Anticipatory Regret motivational messages that express the possibility of regret about future actions.

performance during a game, a coach needs to take care to help keep his or her athletes' emotional arousal at the optimal level to help produce the desired outcome (Martin, 2008).

WHAT THIS MEANS FOR SPORT COMMUNICATION

To be able to convey a sense of ability to play and an enjoyment of a sport is both the easiest and one of the most difficult tasks a coach, parent, or mentor can undertake. This is because the dual components of immediacy and efficacy must work together in order to build physical strength, understanding of the game, and the mental toughness that is necessary for athletic success at different levels of play. The ability to cultivate an understanding of sport includes the need to criticize the actions of the athlete. This includes critiques of both positive and negative behaviors. For example, if ath-

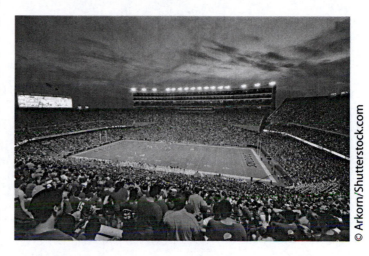

letes are doing a drill correctly, the coach will obviously have positive feedback for the team. If the team is executing the drill, but not very well, the coach will have to give negative feedback by way of corrections to show the team how to improve their performance on the drill. Combining the two messages will help to counter the negative effects of the corrections, if necessary.

The feedback that is sent can help with the growth of self-efficacy, coaching efficacy, and team efficacy; however, without the sense of immediacy, it could hurt the overall relationship between the sender and receiver in the communication. The presence of immediacy is not an absolute deal maker as the players begin to understand the role of the coach, and the communication that is needed to improve and move to the next level. Some athletes just want to know what is necessary to win, and can take the relationships that are formed on the team as the emotional support they need to continue to play. For example, the members of the "Miracle on Ice" 1980 Men's US Olympic Hockey Team did not have an immediate relationship with head coach Herb Brooks, but they completed the greatest upset in Olympic history when they beat the Soviet National Team in their semi-final match up (Witnify, 2014). These men played Division I men's hockey at some of the best colleges in the nation. They did not need a friend in their coach; they needed a leader who could show them how to win. Brooks was that leader, and they respected the situation as it was. However, as athletes are just starting in amateur sports, immediacy is an important tool for all those involved in the growth of the new athlete (Witnify, 2014). This is where communication and sports need to merge to create the most favorable situation for both the coach and the athlete.

DISCUSSION QUESTIONS

1. How important has the coach-athlete relationship been in your personal experience?
2. Can vicarious experiences help build self-efficacy?
3. Though there is danger in the use of regret messages, how can they be regulated for positive use?

REFERENCES

Amorose, A.J., & Weiss, M.R. (1998). Coaching feedback as a source of information about perceptions of ability: A developmental examination. *Journal of Sport and Exercise Psychology, 20,* 395–420.

Bandura, A. (1977). Self-efficacy: Towards a unifying theory of behavioral change. *Psychological Review, 84,* 191–215.

Bandura, A. (1997). *Self-efficacy: The exercise of control.* New York: Freeman.

Black, S.J., & Weiss, M.R. (1992). The relationship among perceived coaching behaviors, perceptions of ability, and motivation in competitive age-group swimmers. *Journal of Sport & Exercise Psychology, 14,* 309–325.

Burke, K., Peterson, D., & Nix, C. (1995). The effects of the coaches' use of humor on female volleyball players' evaluation of their coaches. *Journal of Sport Behavior, 18,* 83–90.

Chelladurai, P. (1984). Discrepancy between preferences and perceptions of leadership behavior and satisfaction of athletes in varying sports. *Journal of Sports Psychology, 6,* 27–41.

Feltz, D.L. & Lirgg, C.D. (1998). Perceived team and player efficacy in hockey. *Journal of Applied Psychology, 83,* 557–564.

Haselwood, D.M., Joyner, A.B., Burke, K.L., Geyerman, C.B., Czech, D.R., Munkasy, B.A., & Zwald, A.D. (2005). Female athletes' perceptions of head coaches' communication competence. *Journal of Sport Behavior, 28,* 216–230.

Hudgins, D., Nevins, D., Aubrey, S., Berg, P., & Grazer, B. (Producers). (2006). *Friday Night Lights* [Television series]. Hollywood: Imagine Entertainment.

Kassing, J.W. & Infante, D.A. (1999). Aggressive communication in the coach-athlete relationship. *Communication Research Reports, 16,* 110–120.

Matsui, T., Kakuyama, T., Onglatco, M.L.U. (1987). Effects of goals and feedback on performance in groups. *Journal of Applied Psychology, 72,* 407–415.

Mehrabian, A. (1972). *Nonverbal communication.* Chicago, IL: Aldine-Atherton.

Myers, N.D., Vargas-Tonsing, T.M., & Feltz, D.L. (2003). Coaching efficacy in intercollegiate coaches: Sources, coaching behavior, and team variables. *Psychology of Sport & Exercise, 6,* 129–143.

Pogue, L.L. & AhYun, K. (2006). The effect of teacher nonverbal immediacy and credibility on student motivation and affective learning. *Communication Education, 55,* 331–344.

Rocca, K.A., Martin, M.M., & Toale, M.C. (1998). Players' perception of their coaches' immediacy, assertiveness, and responsiveness. *Communication Research Reports, 15,* 445–450.

Richmond, V.P. & McCroskey, J.C. (2000). The impact of supervisor and subordinate immediacy on relational organizational outcomes. *Communication Monographs, 67,* 85–95.

Richmond, V.P., McCroskey, J.C., & Johnson, A.D. (2003). Development of the nonverbal immediacy scale (NIS): Measures of self-and other-perceived nonverbal immediacy. *Communication Quarterly, 51,* 504–517.

Turman, P.D. (2003). Athletic coaching from an instructional communication perspective: The influence of coach experience on high school wrestlers' preferences and perceptions of coaching behaviors across a season. *Communication Education, 52,* 72–86.

Turman, P.D. (2005). Coaches' use of anticipatory and counterfactual regret messages during competition. *Journal of Applied Communication Research, 33,* 116–138.

Turman, P.D. & Schrodt, P. (2004). New avenues for instructional communication research: Relationships among coaches' leadership behaviors and athletes' affective learning. *Communication Research Reports, 21*(2), 130–143.

Vargas-Tonsing, T.M., Myers, & Feltz, D.L. (2004). Coaches' and athletes' perception of efficacy-enhancing techniques. *The Sport Psychologist, 18,* 397–414.

Vargas-Tonsing, T.M. & Bartholomew, J.B. (2006). An exploratory study of the effects of pregame speeches on team efficacy beliefs. *Journal of Applied Social Psychology, 36,* 918–933.

Voepel, M. (2007, Sept. 3). WNBA finals matchup already bursting with story lines. Retrieved March 7, 2008. from http:// sports.espn.go.com

Weigand, D.A. & Stockham, K.J. (2000). The importance of analyzing position-specific self-efficacy. *Journal of Sport Behavior, 23,* 61–69.

Westre, K.R. & Weiss, M.R. (1991). The relationship between perceived coaching behaviors and group cohesion in high school football teams. *The Sport Psychologist, 5,* 41–54.

Witnify (2014). The 1980 miracle on ice: Herb Brooks, http://www.sbnation.com/miracle-on-ice-1980-us-hockey/2014/2/11/5400156/the-1980-miracle-on-ice-herb-brooks, Retrieved January 20, 2014.

Bad girls reign over the palace on first day of July, http://www.wnba.com/shock/news/badgirls_050628.html, Retrieved March 7, 2008.

Detroit Shock add Rick Mahorn to coaching staff, http://www.wnba.com/shock/news/rickmahorn_assistantcoach.html, Retrieved March 7, 2008.

CHAPTER 3

FAMILY COMMUNICATION IN SPORT

Chapter Objectives

At the end of this chapter, readers will be able to:

1. Give an example of how parental support of a young athlete can be interpreted by the child as pressure to perform.

2. List three factors CMM evaluates in a communication event.

3. Distinguish between rules-based perspective and laws-based perspective.

4. Describe how a parent can use listening and accommodation to support their child in a sport activity.

Key Terms

Communication accommodation theory	Rules-based perspective	Social norms
Coordinated management of meaning	Laws-based perspective	Mastery climate
	Convergence	Ego climate
	Divergence	

INTRODUCTION

Usually when people think of sports parents, the image of the "typical soccer mom," or dad, comes to mind along with the minivan full of sports gear, excited children, and ice chests filled with Capri Sun or Gatorade and orange slices. It is so common that, for years, manufactures of minivans and sport utility vehicles have been using these images to sell automobiles. The reason these marketing campaigns work is because, for most families, the commercials depict the truth. Often sports provide a positive atmosphere for family interaction, and for life-long enjoyment of sports and activity. Unfortunately, however, this is not always the experience for youth sports participants.

© Artisticco/Shutterstock.com

SPORTS AND FAMILIES

Stories of over-involved parents either causing emotional distress for their children or causing problems for others at youth sporting events is becoming more and more prevalent. From Wanda Holloway who tried to have the mother of her daughter's junior high school cheerleading rival murdered (Lang & Mascia, 2012), to Thomas Junta, the hockey dad who beat the father of another youth hockey player after the young boy landed a rough check on Junta's son during a scrimmage (cbsnews.com), some parents are taking youth sports too seriously. When stories of these parents' behaviors become public, it casts a negative shadow upon youth sports and all the positives that can come from participating in athletics. These atypical parental behaviors are strong juxtapositions to the supportive behaviors of most youth sport parents, such as Debbie Phelps. Watching Debbie Phelps watch her son, Olympic swimmer Michael Phelps, during one of his races, it is clear that she is watching her son swim, not an Olympic athlete in an event.

Being a parent of a young athlete usually provides an opportunity for growth within the relationship between parents and their children (Snyder & Purdy, 1982). Often parents will introduce their child to a variety of extra-curricular activities with the expectation that he or she will find an activity he or she enjoys, have the opportunity to make friends, or even just stay in shape. Some parents hope their children will enjoy the same activities as they enjoyed during their youth. When Debbie Phelps was a young single parent looking to find an activity for a rambunctious young Michael, she never imagined that swimming would become a career for him (Winerip, 2008). When his success became eminent, continuing to pursue his goal of Olympic gold was his decision (Winerip, 2008). When Michael decided to retire from Olympic competition, Debbie once again voiced her support for her son (Winerip, 2008). Throughout his career, Debbie has always be able to communicate her support to Michael in a manner that expressed that she was interested in what was best for her son and that swimming and success were not a condition for her support. Not all parents are able to do the same for their athletes. The similarities between support and smothering of a child by a parent often can be linked to how a parent communicates his or her support (Winerip, 2008). While Debbie Phelps is able to differentiate her message clearly, some other parents seem to have difficulty in the task.

Winning is Everything

One of the prominent storylines from season three of the television series *Friday Night Lights* was that of J.D. McCoy, a freshman quarterback touted as one of the top newcomers in Texas that season. The story of J.D. is one of pressure and privilege (Berg, Aubrey, Nevins, Katims, Reiner, & Hudgins, D. 2011). J.D.'s father, Joe McCoy, is a wealthy Texas businessman who spares no expense to help give his son every opportunity to become the best football player in the state (Berg, et al., 2011). When Joe moved his family to Dillon so he could play for the Panthers,

© Mitch Gunn/Shutterstock.com

he moved J.D.'s private football coach along with the family to help make sure that J.D. had the opportunity to become the starting quarterback. The way Joe saw it, if J.D. earned the role of the coveted "QB 1" of the best high school football team in Texas, he would have to opportunity to play football at a Division I university and possibly play professional football. Just like most parents, Joe McCoy wanted to provide his son with the opportunities to make his dreams come true. However, as the season progresses, viewers see that, along with the privilege and opportunity that his father has provided, comes great pressure for J.D. to perform up to his father's expectations (Berg, et al., 2011).

The experiences of the character of J.D. McCoy are the same that many young athletes experience as they start to progress through their sports career. From the dynamic between J.D. and his father, to that of the young man and his mother who just wants her son to have a normal high school experience, to J.D. having to take direction from two coaches sending him two different messages, the troubles that J.D. experiences exemplify just how communication can shape similar relationships in very different directions (Berg, et al., 2011). Though most athletes do not have as many individuals giving feedback or support as this fictional character does, it is clear how young people can experience conflict when trying to differentiate the support messages communicated to them as individuals from those tied to the support they receive as athletes (Berg, et al., 2011).

How a parent communicates their support can mean the difference between a positive or negative experience for young athletes in sports (Eynon, Kitchen, & Semotick, 1980; Green & Chalip, 1997; Synder & Purdy, 1982). It is important that the parents and athletes understand what each individual wants to come from the child's participation in sports. For example, if parents are spending large sums of money for their child to have expensive equipment and attend expensive camps, because they perceive that is what makes their child happy, this needs to be explained to their young athlete (Eynon, et al., 1980; Green & Chalip, 1997). As stated earlier, if the athlete believes that a parent's approval or love is contingent upon their performance on the playing field, this can cause undue anxiety for the athlete. A misunderstanding of a situation, miscommunication, or simply a misunderstanding of the behaviors of either party and therefore a lack of communication usually causes these situations. Coordinated Management of Meaning (CMM) is a theory that works to explain how parents can create an understanding of social perspective for children (Pearce & Cronen, 1980). This theory can be used in sport settings to explain how children develop sports affiliation, the importance of sports involvement, and as explained here, expectations of parents as to the child's level of participation in sports.

COORDINATED MANAGEMENT OF MEANING

The basic core of communication is hinged on the concept that every word spoken has a special meaning to the sender and to the receiver. This meaning is dependent on several factors, such as history of past communication and social factors such as age, relationship of individuals, and overall context of the conversation, to name a few (Berlo, 1960; McCroskey, 1968). Considering how much can go wrong in a conversation leading to miscommunication, it seems surprising that we are so often able to create accurate meaning in the conversations in which we engage. **Coordinated Management of Meaning (CMM)** seeks to explain how we are able to successfully create meaning (Pearce & Cronen, 1980).

CMM is a rules-based theory that is often used in family communication to help explain how parental communication can influence the societal perspectives of their children (Philipsen, 1995). A **rules-based perspective**, in contrast to a **laws-based approach**, gives weight to an individual's ability to make choices based on the rules, or norms, that are common in each society (Pearce & Wiseman, 1983). This paradigm is a contrast to the laws perspective, or paradigm, which sees communication-based behaviors as more predetermined or mechanical; essentially more predicated on the outside forces that influence behavior (i.e., culture, environment, context) and less by the individual. Though the use of social norms in the rules perspective may make it appear to fall under the laws paradigm, the rules perspective focuses on the *individual* and the rules of the *situation* guiding the communication interaction, and not the larger society as a whole (Pearce & Wiseman, 1983). For example, the norms/rules of one family may differ from those of the neighbor's family; and both would have different rules than what the children of each family would expect to follow at school or with their sports teams. Each of these different groups in the example are considered individually under the rules perspective. Rules are learned through either observing them in society, or through direct explanation (Pearce

Coordinated Management of Meaning a theory which seeks to explain how we are able to successfully create meaning.

Rules-based perspective an individual's ability to make choices based on the rules, or norms, that are common in each society.

Laws-based perspective views communication-based behaviors as more predetermined or mechanical; more predicated on the outside forces that influence behavior.

& Wiseman, 1983). For example, a coach may state what the rules of the team are; however, how or in what manner the rules are to be followed or enacted can only be learned through observation. How a drill is to be run by a team is only an exercise on paper until these drills are run during practice and the athletes are able to understand what a coach envisions for the drill. Even more to the point, transitions between drills (i.e., the time it is expected to take to move from one drill to another, who leads which drill, who signals, the beginning and ending of a drill, etc.) are also a norm that is learned both through explanation and observation.

Coordinated Management of Meaning looks to evaluate understanding based on the behavioral output of the communication versus a word-for-word determination of meaning (Pearce & Cronen, 1980). Essentially, if the conversation results in the expected (or sought after) outcome, it does not matter if the individuals achieved 100% understanding of each word communicated, the essence of the message was understood. CMM focuses on three factors in an outcome: Have the individuals (1) decoded the messages with enough (2) understanding to create an (3) outcome that is satisfactory to the intent of the communication purpose? If the answer to this question is yes, then coordination of the meaning of the message has been achieved (Pearce & Cronen, 1980). If the answer is no, communication must persist until the purpose of the interaction has been successfully achieved.

From a communication perspective, this seems to indicate an ability to avoid the pitfalls of miscommunication from the example in the beginning of this section. However, this is not necessarily the case. As stated before, there is always the chance that coordination of communicated messages will not take place. This means that misunderstanding is always a possible outcome. In sports, this can look like a perfect "steal" signal sent from a third base coach executed by the runners on third (coordination), or an interception thrown for a pick six because the quarterback called for a post route and the receiver ran a slant to the corner (non-coordination). Sporting events have a multitude of opportunities for CMM to be demonstrated. Family communication, however, can be little more difficult to describe.

PARENT-CHILD COMMUNICATION

The coordination of meaning in a conversation is not only a matter of decoding cues to understand the messages being sent between the individuals in the conversation. It is understood that communication entails much more than just the conversation that is happening in the moment (Pearce & Cronen, 1980) Factors that influence the current conversation include the environment in which the conversation is taking place, past history between the communication partners, internal and external noise, as well as a general lack of shared meaning (Pearce & Cronen, 1980). How cues are decoded is dependent upon the social constructs of the conversation, as well (Pearce & Cronen, 1980). These constructs are what create the perceived social reality that exists within each and every conversation (Pearce & Cronen, 1980).

Past History Matters

The first tenet of CMM states that realities between individuals are built upon the experiences of the individuals during the conversation (focusing on the conversational content) as well as the experiences between the individuals engaging in the conversation (Pearce & Cronen, 1980). Past history has a way of playing a role in current communication, regardless of whether or not individuals intend to bring the past into the current conversation (Pearce & Cronen, 1980).

Referring back to the initial example of Mr. McCoy and young J.D., parent-child communication needs to be focused on support in sports and not be centered only on the young athlete's success. Without this differentiation the parent-child dynamic risks being overtaken by the child's participation in sport. For example, assume a parent complained in front of his or her child about the cost of sport participation when first signing their child up for a sport. Now assume that the league was not being run properly, or that the coach of the team was consistently canceling practice or not attending games. In this situation, the parent would probably be upset because he or she did not believe that his or her child was receiving the experience or the opportunity to learn that was anticipated when originally registering for the league. If the parent simply complained about the overall experience and did not voice his or her disappointment on behalf of his or her athlete but rather just to or in front of the athlete, the child may not understand the message as the parent intended (Collins & Barber, 2005). This misunderstanding would be based on the parent's past complaints of cost for the league and the equipment, as well as their current complaints of "not getting their money's worth" from the season. The child may believe that he or she is being a financial burden on the family and the parent is angry about it. If the child does not understand the actual context for the parent's complaints about the value of the experience, the next time he or she wants to play a sport, there may be hesitation in the request, or a complete lack of a request.

Say It How You Mean It

The second tenet of CMM refers to the old adage of what one says is not as important as how one says it (Pearce & Cronen, 1980). Part of creating our social reality includes the manner in which the conversation will always influence the reality of the communication (Pearce & Cronen, 1980). How often has it happened that what started off as a peaceful conversation evolves into a conflict because of the tone or behavior of one, or both, of the individuals in the conversation? Moving the examples away from parents to the family dynamic that can exist between teammates and between coaches and athletes, imagine the scenario of a coach having to put a player on the bench due to injury; the conversation between player and coach can happen in a couple of different ways. First the coach can approach the player expressing concern for the health and future of the player, creating a positive outlook to the current negative situation. The coach could also express the frustration common in these situations which could alter the perception of the athlete, making an already negative situation worse. Though the coach could be frustrated at the situation, as injury can alter the course of a season, if the coach does not show concern for the athlete along with the concern for the team, the relationship between the coach and athlete could suffer irreconcilable damage.

This situation is true in family communication, as well. Assume the same injury scenario in a family setting. If parents can communicate their concern for the wellbeing of their child as much as their concern for the wellbeing for the team, the messages will have a better opportunity of being processed and understood by the athlete. If there is a question of whether or not the parent is more concerned with what the injury means to the future of the team than the effect on the child, there is opportunity for miscommunication, and the end result can be damaging to the relationship between the parent and the athlete. It can also damage the athlete's interest in sports if they believe, as was explained in the scenario in the beginning of the chapter, that their parent's approval is contingent upon successful sports performance (Collins & barber, 2005).

BACK TO FRIDAY NIGHT . . .

As the season of *Friday Night Lights* progresses, we see Coach Taylor make the decision to start playing J.D. over Matt Saracen, a decision that works well for the Dillon Panthers and J.D. McCoy the quarterback; however, as viewers start to realize, is not in J.D. the high school freshman's best interest. Joe McCoy states that all of his efforts are meant to please his son and help J.D. realize his dreams; however, it seems as if Joe is much harder to please than his son (Berg, et al., 2011). Though J.D. is a football phenom, a freshman with talent beyond his years, off the field he is a just a typical freshman. He is shy, starting to get more and more interested in girls, and trying to fit in at his new high school. Just like other kids his age, J.D. wants to go to parties, hang out with friends, and just live a normal teenage life. Joe has other plans for his son. As J.D. starts to pay attention to things other than football, Joe starts to resist his son's interests in a "real life" until after football season is over. His messages to J.D. start to become more and more "clear" . . . football is more important than his son. Joe tells his son that fun and girls will still be there after football season is over and that J.D. should just wait on everything until then.

Back in the Day

When we first see father and son together, the McCoy men look like the epitome of father-son perfection. They joke, talk sports, and appear to have a strong relationship. The McCoy home even has a trophy room with all of J.D.'s awards and sports photos on display. This all starts to change as Joe starts to pressure his son to work harder, try more, and be perfect on and off the field, and push his personal life aside. As Joe's negative behavior starts to increase, so does J.D.'s rebellion including hiding his relationship with his girlfriend and sneaking out to parties. The communication between father and son begins to disintegrate quickly as both individuals seem to be working to be heard over the other. J.D. perceives his father as only interested in having a son who is a football star, and

Joe sees J.D. as throwing away his potential and future. As a teenager with growing popularity, J.D. does not realize that high school football is not the end of the road but rather the beginning, and Joe does not realize that at 15, young men often cannot see past the parties and popularity that come with being a small town football hero. Father and son need to speak each other's language.

COMMUNICATION ACCOMMODATION THEORY

Communication Accommodation Theory extension of SAT that accounts for both verbal and nonverbal behaviors of the communication partners.

Convergence defined as the behaviors that one individual partakes in as a means to accommodate their communication partner.

Divergence behaviors that one individual partakes in when they make sure to accentuate the differences through their lack of adaptation to behaviors of their communication partners.

One of the biggest issues in the relationship between the McCoys is Joe's and J.D.'s inability to understand what the other truly wants. This can happen for several reasons, one of which is the basic lack of listening, hearing, and responding. **Communication Accommodation Theory (CAT)** was developed out of the growth of **Speech Accommodation Theory (SAT)** as a means to help explain the behavior of communication partners through the factors of convergence and divergence (Giles, Coupland, & Coupland, 1991). To fully understand CAT, one must first understand SAT. SAT (Giles, 1973) first investigated the concepts of association and disassociation through the behaviors individuals displayed in conversation. These behaviors include accent changes as a means of either convergence or divergence. **Convergence** is defined as the behaviors that one individual partakes in as a means to accommodate their communication partner (Giles, 1973). Convergence occurs when one, or both, individual(s) are attempting to show that he or she, or both, are interested in continuing future interactions. According to SAT, convergent behaviors include word choice and change of accent (Giles, 1973). **Divergent behavior** is the opposite of convergent behavior, in that it is intended to stop a conversation, or at least guarantee that future conversations will not take place. When individuals do not want to continue to interact with others, they make sure to accentuate the differences through their lack of adaptation to behaviors of their communication partners (Giles, 1973). The purpose of SAT was to explain what benefits, or consequences, would result from individuals displaying convergent or divergent behavior.

Giles (1973) focused his research on finding out how people display the communication behaviors that are specific to either diverging or converging, as well as why they would opt to do so. This included behaviors such as accent changes to either seem similar or different from his or her partner. Behaviors not associated with direct verbal communication can also influence how a person chooses to communicate, based on the perception of one's environment (Giles, 1973). The perception of one's environment influences accommodation or non-accommodation as it influences one's choice of behavior, tone, word choice, as well as depth of conversation, just to name a few elements of communication. An example of this would be the choice of language a parent may use towards his or her child in front of a coach versus how they would speak in private. A parent who may not agree with a coach's decision may express his or her feelings when the coach is not around, or other teammates are not around; however, in public, he or she may side with the coach so as to not cause problems for his or her child.

These behavioral changes based on environment are often referred to as "social norms," which was also a focus of Giles (1973) and the Speech

Accommodation Theory. **Social norms** are defined as the "rules" for behavior that individuals adhere to based on what they are taught as normal or acceptable for the setting (Pearce & Wiseman, 1983). Therefore, communication behaviors often hinge upon the situation, or setting, in which they are being displayed. These behaviors can vary from whispering while in a library, to following traffic rules to avoid getting a ticket or arrested, to following the rules of a sport being played. Golf is a perfect example of enacting social norms in sports; players are expected to be honest by following the rules and keeping the correct score. If this does not happen, the player will be disqualified. There is also the negative perception that is associated with not following the rules as it is often seen as cheating. Just as ignoring this social norm will cause others not to trust the golfer, not following communicative social norms will cause individuals to not want to continue to speak with their communication partner.

Social norms hinge upon the context, situation, and environment in which the individual is communicating and in which the behavior is being enacted; therefore, they are not behavioral norms that are standard over a series of situations, but rather they are fluid and flow from one condition to the next. Because of this, norms can often dictate how a person should behave rather than allowing the individual to act as he or she prefers to act. However, as has been seen on many occasions, not everyone follows the predetermined social norms.

SAT eventually grew enough for a new theory, communication accommodation theory (CAT), allowing for the new theory to account for both verbal and nonverbal behaviors of the communication partners. One factor that both theories maintained is the concept of intent. Though the decision to either converge or diverge is not always intentional, it can be based on a conscious decision. Most are aware of their behavior and the goal of enacting behaviors for a desired result; however, individuals can make themselves appear similar or dissimilar without realizing they are doing so. For example, take a look at the situation a new teammate could experience when first starting with a team. The individual would obviously want to be accepted by his or her new teammates, so they would look to start conversations with the team to show them that he or she is good enough to play the sport and, hopefully, be accepted by the other players. In his or her attempt to seem similar, he or she may follow stories about athletic accomplishment that other teammates share with one of his or her own. Though the goal is to show they he or she is just as good as the other players on the team, it may just alienate the new teammates by being perceived as bragging. Though the intent was convergence, the result was divergence. He or she may be seen as rude or a show-off, thereby causing him or her to stand out rather than blend in.

SAT worked to help researchers predict and explain how individuals used verbal messages, both in content and certain nonverbal cues, to indicate intent to continue or terminate communication with an other individual. CAT worked to expand the depth of the theory by expanding the focus of nonverbal behaviors used in either process (Giles, 2008; Giles, Coupland, & Coupland, 1991). The concept of convergence in communication under CAT expanded with the growth of the theory to include factors such as speech rate, and the length of

Social norms defined as the "rules" for behavior that individuals adhere to based on what they are taught as normal or acceptable for the setting.

one's utterances, along with pauses in communication, gaze, phonological variants, and smiling (Giles, Coupland, & Coupland, 1991). This change allows for the theory to better answer questions of how and why convergence/divergence occurs.

According to Giles (2008), differences are reduced through accommodation "by enhancing interpersonal similarities and thereby reducing uncertainty about the other" (p. 163). The level of accommodation is crucial to the effectiveness of the attempt. Essentially, if you seem too similar, or not similar enough, the attempt at accommodation will look fake, and divergence will be the end result. This is what happened in the example of the new player on the team presented earlier in the chapter. As stated earlier, divergence is used as an attempt to ensure that communication will not continue. The behaviors enacted during divergence are done so as to make differences salient and to ensure that they are obvious to the other speaker. If the differences become obvious, and communication ends, then "mission accomplished."

The process of converging or diverging is usually associated with the process of reducing uncertainty (during convergence) as a means of creating understanding between two individuals. When seeing CAT from the perspective of family communication, the purpose of convergence and divergence in the parent-child relationship needs a focus.

PARENTS AND SPORTS

When parents first get their children involved in sports they do so for a multitude of reasons. From Debbie Phelps' story of a hyper Michael who needed an outlet (Winerp, 2008) to the fictional tale of the McCoys and a father wanting to grow the potential of his only son (Berg, et al., 2011), whatever the reason, the entry of a child into organized sports is a learning process for both the parent and the athlete (Snyder & Purdy, 1982). According to Dorsch, Smith, and McDonough (2009), "parents' changes in behavioral cognition, and affect that occurs as a result of the organizational sport participation of their children" (p. 446) is akin to a socialization process. So an understanding of social norms centered on sports grows from experiences in sports itself, and from these norms grow communication processes that would allow parents to communicate about the particular sport with their child and others involved.

This understanding of proper communication and behaviors within a sport setting is especially important for families, as the number of children and teenagers playing organized sports has been growing exponentially over the past several years (Kelley & Carchia, 2013). In 2009, the *Columbus Dispatch* reported an estimated $5 billion were generated by non-profit sports organizations ranging from the Amateur Athletic Union (AAU) to neighborhood sports leagues (Kelley & Carchia, 2013). Seeing this report, ESPN furthered the investigation in an attempt to calculate just how many young kids in America were involved in organized sports in order to generate this amount of annual revenue (Kelley & Carchia, 2013). What they found was an inability to come close to calculating a number that was near accurate, as many of the leagues did not need to report any of their records to an organizing committee (i.e., neighborhood leagues do not report to Little League, martial arts academies, etc.). However, even with this lack of official records, the numbers that ESPN were able to estimate based on the data that was available found that youth sports participation ranged from 21 to 28 million athletes every year (Kelley & Carchia, 2013). Though the number is assumed to be accurate, the estimates were for individuals between the ages of 6 and 17; this left a large demographic out of the equation as many children start organized sports before the age of 6 (Kelley & Carchia, 2013). Because sport participation can have a strong impact on the family dynamic, an understanding of how communication can, and should, take place within the family dynamic about sport participation is crucial to a positive experience for all involved.

SOCIAL LEARNING OF SPORT

Fans of the show *Big Bang Theory* probably remember the episode in season three, "The Cornhusker Vortex" where Penny invites Leonard to watch the Nebraska Cornhuskers game with her and her friends (Lorre, et al., 2009). This would seem like a normal Saturday event for a couple; however, Leonard has no knowledge of football teams, rules, or social norms. The event turns out to be an embarrassing for Leonard and Penny, even though he tries to act like he knows what is happening in the

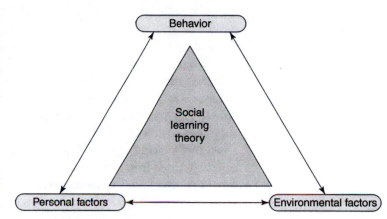

game. Though Sheldon teaches Leonard the rules, there is more to participating with the group than just knowing what is happening on TV. This is the same with parents trying to communicate with their children about their sports, as well as the others involved in the sport environment.

Though many parents have played sports in the past, they may not have played every sport their child is currently involved in. This means that, in order to fully participate in this part of their child/children's lives, mom and/or dad will need to learn about this "new" sport. As mentioned earlier, the child's participation also often means that parents have to invest a substantial amount of money into equipment and registration in order for their child to be able to play, depending on the sport, of course (Eynon, Kitchen, & Semotick, 1980; Green & Chalip, 1997). This investment of money and time usually sparks a natural interest in many different aspects of their athlete's participation (Synder & Purdy, 1982). These include the enjoyment levels of their child in the sport, the success of the team, the leadership and behaviors of the coach, and the overall performance of their child in the sport, to name a few (Synder & Purdy, 1982). To find out this information, parents often can have conversations about the team and the progress of the season with their child. They can go to games to see how the team and the coach are performing, ask about practices, and may even engage other parents during events for the team. They can read or watch sports to learn more about the game. Though this behavior is often seen as a positive family bonding opportunity by the parents and the children involved, if it is not executed in the proper manner, it can be something that can hurt the family relationships involved (Dorsch, et al., 2009; O'Rourke, Smith, & Smoll, 2011).

Through this process, it is obvious that parents are showing interest in their children and their children's team; however, how this interest is communicated needs to be monitored just as closely as parents monitor communication about other topics in their child's life (Dorsch, et al., 2009). O'Rourke, Smith, & Smoll (2011) sought to determine how motivational efforts on behalf of parents influenced the anxiety levels of their children during sport participation. They found that parents who engage their young athletes about performance-based goals, including increasing effort, learning from his or her mistakes, and improving his or her skill could adversely be creating anxiety instead of actually encouraging their child (O'Rourke, et al., 2011). The study focused on two types of sport-based motivational climates, *mastery* and *ego* (p. 400). The **mastery climate** is defined as the condition where "effort, enjoyment, and self-improvement are emphasized, mistakes are not punished but viewed as a medium for learning, and the criteria for success is self-influenced instead of being based on social comparison" (O'Rourke, et al., 2011, p. 400). In this environment, athletes are able to learn, not only from practice and play, but also from the mistakes that they make without risking feeling like a failure, or increasing anxiety levels as a result of playing a game. **Ego climate** is the motivational climate where "success is defined in terms of outperforming others using equal or less effort and mistakes are viewed as unacceptable and punished" (O'Rourke, et al., 2011, p. 400). In this climate, athletes are concerned with both the perfection of playing a sport as well as the effort needed to better their opponents.

O'Rourke, et al. (2011) found that a focus on mastery versus ego climate could reduce the anxiety felt by an athlete because, as those who participated in their study indicated that they felt more control over their ability to improve their play in comparison to their own previous efforts. Their focus was on overall improvement of their skills and understanding of the sport, not on winning alone. Athletes are also able to control factors of personal improvement versus the work their teammates are putting in to improve their own skills. Because ego climate motivation requires the athlete to out-perform another in order to gauge improvement in a sport, the athlete feels less control over their success as it is dependent upon the performances of other athletes, and different athletes each and every game/match. Because the level of control in ego climates is limited, the athlete's level of anxiety is increased (O'Rourke, et al., 2011).

When considering how parents attempt to motivate their children, they need to be aware of how the communication takes place, as creating an ego climate versus a motivational climate could be detrimental to the enjoyment level of the athlete, as well as the longevity of sport participation for their child. Parents need to be especially cognizant of the level of pressure that his or her child can withstand before the young athlete begins to resent the attention a parent gives to his or her sport participation (Lee & MacLean, 1997). For example,

Mastery climate defined as the condition where "effort, enjoyment, and self-improvement are emphasized, mistakes are not punished but viewed as a medium for learning.

Ego climate the motivational climate where "success is defined in terms of outperforming others using equal or less effort and mistakes are viewed as unacceptable and punished".

though pushing a child to "finish what they start" is a good life lesson, if the child is unhappy in their sports, this may turn into resentment rather than a positive life lesson. Another example comes from Sapieja, Dunn, and Hold (2011): parents often spend a large amount of time and money in order for their children to participate in sports, and a focus on success rather than learning can often send the wrong message indicating to athletes that their parents want a return on their investment.

THE BATTLE OF THE MCCOY MEN

The example that best describes the difference between a parent accommodating their communication to the needs of their child and a parent who does not is evident in the example from *Friday Night Lights* (Berg, et al., 2011) that was described in the beginning of this chapter. As was stated earlier, Joe McCoy wanted what was best for his son, J.D., but the manner in which he expressed his support showed more divergence than convergence in his communication; or, perhaps, more ego motivation versus mastery motivation. When J.D. was on the field, Joe knew exactly how to "talk sports" with his son. He made sure he had the right coaches, played at the right schools, and had the right equipment to help him pursue his dreams. When they stepped off the field, Joe the sports father never really transitioned to Joe the dad. His communication continued to be focused on J.D.'s future as a college and professional quarterback rather than his life as a teenager in high school. It is clear from watching the show that the character of Joe wanted to be viewed as the "cool father" who talked sports, hung out with his son, wanted a connection to his son's life and wanted to help J.D. in any way he could. As the television season, and fictional football season, progresses we see that the young quarterback begins to see the communication from his father as more ego driven and contingent on his success with the Dillon Panthers. According to Lee and MacLean (1997), communication about a child's participation in sports is necessary, but only to the extent that the support is not perceived as an attempt to take control of the experience of the athlete. In the show *Friday Night Lights*, the support that Joe McCoy gives to his son in the show would be ideal; however, because the father-son relationship is so focused on the current and future success of the athlete and not on the family dynamic, J.D. perceives his father's love as connected to his performance on the football field. The anxiety level for the young QB reaches its pinnacle and the two McCoy men end up fighting in a parking lot after a football game.

SUPPORT OF A YOUNG ATHLETE: LISTENING AND ACCOMMODATION

So the question becomes, how can parents understand how much support is too much support? Or, in the terms of CAT, when does support shift from convergence to divergence? According to several studies, inappropriate parental communication can include putting too much emphasis on winning (i.e., Joe

McCoy) and being overly critical when critiquing performances, which in turn can result in excessive pressure to perform, fear of failure, lower perceived competence, as well as sport-based competitive anxiety (Bois, Lalanne, & Delforge, 2009; Leff & Hoyle, 1995; Sagar & Lavallee, 2010). The best solution is to listen and communicate along the lines that the athlete sets out or to accommodate to meet the needs to the athlete. To help parents achieve this, they need to create an open and clear line of communication that allows the child to tell them about his or her experiences in sports, his or her enjoyment levels, and what he or she would like to achieve.

Dorsch, et al. (2009) suggest that sports was able to provide more options for communication among parents and children in their study, and that parents will be able to have successful sport relationships with their children when they "look to their children for emotional cues and adjust their emotional reactions to match" (p. 456). Though this concept may seem obvious, a study from Jones (2002) indicates that often, parents and coaches alike are not always in tune to what athletes are looking for when they are participating in a sport. According to the study, which focused on the perceived athlete enjoyment of several different aspects of a summer soccer camp, coaches and parents alike misinterpreted what parts of the camp the children were most interested in. The athletes participating in the summer camp listed playing games and learning skills as the activity they enjoyed the most in camp; however, parents and coaches both listed learning in general as the most enjoyable factor for the athletes (Jones, 2002). In contrast, parents ranked games and skills as third and coaches listed it as fourth on their top five list. Athletes listed learning focus as fourth on their top five. The rest of the list continued to show inconsistencies between parent, coach, and athlete perceptions. Parents clearly saw camp as an educational experience, as did the coaches. Athletes, however, saw playing a sport, having fun off the field, and hanging out with friends as more important. This study supports the assumption for youth athletes that sports are based mainly on fun, not future potential. It also supports the idea that not all parents have the same understanding as their athletes as to why the young person wants to play sports. Because of this, parents need to listen to what their child enjoys about being an athlete and learn to accommodate their communication accordingly.

WHAT THIS MEANS FOR SPORT COMMUNICATION

Communication is important, as athletes need strong support from their parents if they are going to continue to participate at higher levels of the game (Monsaas, 1985). Examples of this are Michael Phelps, as demonstrated in the beginning of the chapter, as well as 2014 NBA MVP Kevin Durant, whose emotional speech at his MVP ceremony showed exactly how much a parent can influence the future of a star athlete. Though parental pressure can predict precompetition anxiety levels (Gould, et al., 1991), athletes who believe their parents' interest, time, and money spent is based on their confidence in their child versus expectations for the future can be of great benefit to the confidence and performance of the young athlete (Collins & Barber, 2005). Ullrich-French and

Smith (2006) and Von Ypren (1995) found that the less support that athletes had from parents and friends, the lower levels of performance and the higher level of stress for both the athlete and the team. This is not to say that some levels of parental pressure to perform will be completely detrimental to the athlete, but according to Sapieja, et al. (2011), the better the relationship with the family outside of sports, the more pressure that can be tolerated by the athlete in a sports environment. So essentially, it all comes back to the relationship off the field being a healthy balance to the relationship on the field.

DISCUSSION QUESTIONS

1. How can communication accommodation theory influence how parents are able to either help or hinder their child's growth in sports? How can it influence how coaches either help or hinder their athlete's growth?

2. In the case of J.D. and Joe McCoy, what could have been done through coordinated management of meaning to help save their father-son relationship?

3. How are the social norms that exist in sports that do not exist in the non-sport environment?

4. How do these different sport social norms usually reveal themselves, how are they learned?

REFERENCES

Berg, P., Aubrey, S., Nevins, D., Katims, S., Reiner, J., & Hudgins, D. (2011). *Friday Night Lights* [Television Series]. Universal City, CA: Universal Media Studios.

Berlo, D.K. (1960). *The process of communication.* New York: Holt, Rinehart & Winston.

Bois, J.E., Lalanne, J., & Delforge, C. (2009). The influence of parenting practices and parental presence on children's and adolescents' pre-competitive anxiety. *Journal of Sport Sciences, 27(10),* 995–1005.

CBSNEWS.com. (2002, January 2). *Hockey dad found guilty.* Retrieved from http://web.archive.org/web/20140415160750/http://www.cbsnews.com/news/hockey-dad-found-guilty/.

Collins, K., & Barber, H. (2005). Female athletes' perception of parental influences. *Journal of Sport Behavior, 28(4),* 295–314.

Dorsch, T.E., Smith, A.L., & McDonough, H. (2009). Parents' perceptions of child-to-parent socialization in organized youth sport. *Journal of Sport and Exercise Psychology, 31,* 444–468.

Eynon, R., Kitchen, P., & Semotiuk, D. (1980). The economics of age-group swimming in Ontario. *Canadian Journal of Applied Sport Sciences, 5,* 132–136.

Giles, H. (1973). Accent mobility: A model and some data. *Anthropological Linguistics, 15,* 87–105.

Giles, H. (2008). Accommodating translational research. *Journal of Applied Communication Research, 36(2),* 121–127.

Giles, H., Coupland, J., & Coupland, N. (1991). Accommodation theory: Communication, context, and consequences. In H. Giles, J. Coupland, & N. Coupland (Eds.), *Contexts of accommodation: Development in applied sociolinguistics.* (pp. 1–68). Cambridge, UK: Cambridge University Press.

Gould, D., Eklund, R.C., Petlichkoff, L., Petersen, K., & Bump, L. (1991). Psychological predictors of state anxiety and performance in age-group wrestlers. *Pediatric Exercise Science, 3,* 198–208.

Green, B.C., & Chalip, L. (1997). Enduring involvement in youth soccer: The socialization of parent and child. *Journal of Leisure Research, 29,* 61–77.

Jones, R. (2002). Summer soccer camp enjoyment: Parent, coach, and child perceptions. *European Journal of Physical Education, 7(1),* 45–62.

Kelley, B., & Carchia, C. (2013). Hey, data data—swing. *ESPN.com.* Retrieved from http://espn.go.com/espn/story/_/id/9469252/hidden-demographics-youth-sports-espn-magazine.

Lang, A., & Mascia, K. (2012, February 20). The Texas cheerleader case: A daughter's painful journey. *People.* 77(8). Retrieved from http://www.people.com/people/archive/article/0,,20571464,00.html.

Lee, M., & MacLean, S. (1997). Sources of parental pressure among age group swimmers. *European Journal of Physical Education, 2,* 167–177.

Leff, S., & Hoyle, R.H. (1995). Young athletes' perceptions of parental support and pressure. *Journal of Youth and Adolescence, 24,* 187–203.

Lorre, C. Prady, B., Geotsch, D., Rosenstock, R., Prady, B., Molaro, S. (Writers), & Cendrowski, M. (Director). The cornhusker vortex [Television series episode]. In Chuck Lorre Productions (Producer), *Big Bang Theory.* Burbank, CA: Warner Bros. Television.

McCroskey, J.C. (1968). *An introduction to rhetorical communication.* Englewood Cliffs, NJ: Prentice-Hall.

Monsaas, J.A. (1985). Learning to be a world-class tennis player. In B.S. Bloom (Ed.). *The development of talent in young people* (pp. 211–269). New York: Ballantine.

O'Rourke, D.J., Smith, R.E., & Smoll, F.L. (2011). Trait anxiety in young athletes as a function of parental pressure and motivational climate: Is parental pressure always harmful? *Journal of Applied Sport Psychology, 23,* 398–412.

Pearce, W.B., & Cronen, V.E. (1980). *Communication, action, and meaning.* New York: Praeger.

Pearce, W.B., & Wiseman, R.L. (1983). Rules theories: Varieties, limitations, and potentials. In W. B. Gudykunst (Ed.), *Intercultural communication theory* (pp. 79–88). Beverly Hills, CA: Sage.

Philipsen, G. (1995). The coordinated management of meaning theory of Pearce, Cronen, and Associates. In D.P. Cushman & B. Kovacic (Eds.), *Watershed research traditions in human communication theory* (pp.13–43). Albany: State University of New York Press.

Sager, S.S., & Lavallee, D. (2010). The developmental origins of feat and failure in adolescent athletes: Examining parental practices. *Psychology of Sport and Exercise, 11,* 177–187.

Sapieja, K.M., Dunn, J.G.H., & Holt, N.L. (2011). Perfectionism and perceptions of parenting styles in male youth soccer. *Journal of Sport & Exercise Psychology, 33,* 20–39.

Snyder, E.E., & Purdy, D.A. (1982). Socialization into sport: Parent and child reverse and reciprocal effects. *Research Quarterly for Exercise and Sport, 53,* 263–266.

Ullrich-French, S., & Smith, A.L. (2006). Perceptions of relationships with parents and peers in youth sport: Independent and combined prediction of motivational outcomes. *Psychology of Sport and Exercise, 7,* 193–214.

Van Yperen, N.W. (1995). Interpersonal stress, performance level, and parental support: A longitudinal study among highly skilled young soccer players. *The Sport Psychologist, 9,* 225–241.

Winerip, M. (2008, August 2). Phelps' mother recalls helping her son find gold-medal focus. *The New York Times.* Retrieved from http://www.nytimes.com/2008/08/10/sports/olympics/10Rparent.html?pagewanted=all&_r=0.

CHAPTER 4

MILLENNIAL ATHLETES

Chapter Objectives

At the end of this chapter, readers will be able to:

1. List three shared experiences that helped shape the Millennial Generation.

2. Give an example of a shared experience and an example of a personal experience that have shaped you as a member of your generation.

3. Explain something that you learned from a previous generation and something that you have learned that you hope to teach to a later generation.

4. List the eight propositions that make up Dyadic Power Theory.

5. Describe how the Millennial Generation has and has not changed the power relationships in sports.

Key Terms

Millennial generation	Hierarchical structure	Relationship level
Theory of generations	Dyadic power theory	understanding
Generation X	(DPT)	Manifest power
Power	Content level understanding	

INTRODUCTION

Generation X Individuals who were born between 1961–1981.

The Silent Generation, The Baby Boomers, **Generation X**, The Millennials. These are all names that scholars and pop culture analysts alike have given to members of society in an attempt to identify and categorize individuals based on age and usually common behaviors. Why do we do this? Why do we pay so much attention to who and what "a generation" may or may not represent? One explanation could be a natural instinct for individuals to categorize individuals or to use stereotypes to help us communicate with one another, especially when we do not have a base of knowledge as to how to communicate with people we do not know (Berger, 1975). Though this could be one explanation, in society we tend to use knowledge about generations for so much more than just a baseline for communication. This chapter will explain how generations are formed, who are the "Millennials" of Generation Y, and how the athletes of this generation have seemed to break away from traditional stereotypes associated with their own generation.

TRYING TO IDENTIFY WHO WE ARE

From *The Breakfast Club* to *Glee*, movies and popular media have been entertaining audiences with stories about groups of young people trying to maneuver their way through life. Usually the best of these movies attempt to frame these stories against a backdrop of an adult world full of grownups who just do not get who these "kids" are. The Hollywood practice of defining who a generation is and what the members of the generation represent has continually made for exciting, and profitable, entertainment for years (just ask the Brat Pack and John Hughes), but it has also become more difficult when the subject is Gen Y (those born between 1982 and 2002). When looking at movies, such as *The Breakfast Club, Reality Bites,* or *Clerks,* one can see a relatively similar and accurate depiction of members of Generation X (those born between 1961 and 1981) as eager, frustrated, hardworking, and ultimately misunderstood by nearly everyone who was not a fellow "Xer" (Hughes, 1985; Smith, 1994; Stiller & Childres, 1994). In *The Breakfast Club*, the characters in the movie come together one Saturday morning for detention, each having gotten in trouble at school for different reasons. The students fit the "typical" high school stereotypes of cool kids, "burn outs," and nerds (Hughes, 1985). Though the students cannot stand each other at first, as the day progresses they find out that each of them has more in common with each other than they thought. Like most of the individuals in a generation, these kids all had different backgrounds and interests, but their concerns for their futures, feelings of insecurity, and anger stemming from being so underestimated by their elders leads them to form a bond that can only come from knowing you are essentially the same (Hughes, 1985). The story of teen angst was a common trend from many movies during the 1980's and 1990's (Hughes, 1985; Smith, 1994; Stiller & Childres, 1994).

MOVIES FOR Y

Fast-forward to movies such as *Social Network* about the advent of Facebook, and the documentary *Restrepo* about the new generation of American soldiers, and you can see that Millennials are not an easy group to categorize (Allers & Minkoff, 1994; bachelorsdegreeonline.com; Fincher, 2010; Hetherington & Junger, 2010). Even television shows such as *Glee* prove how it is hard to pinpoint one stereotype of this generation to each character; instead they have successfully worked to identify each "type" of Millennial who is doing his or her part to shape not only his or her own world but society as a whole (Woodall, Novick, Silverstein, Del Valle, & Aguire-Sacasa, 2009).

The students at the fictional McKinley High School are not the angry loners that one would see in the Gen X movies mentioned earlier. The *Glee* characters do not often have the struggle with authority that Generation X characters had to experience. Where "Xers" were constantly seen as trying to get their elders to view them as worthy of trust, responsibility, and respect, the characters in Millennial movies are often showered with praise and more respect than their generational predecessors could have ever imagined (Howe & Strauss, 1993). This leads many to ask why, just one generation apart, are the experiences of these two groups so different? To answer this question, it is first necessary to understand how generations are conceptually structured, and second what exactly is a "Millennial."

© Randy Miramontez/Shutterstock.com

STARTING TO DEFINE THE AGES

Every generation will have events that shape who they are. Wars, politics, pop culture, the economy—these are all events that have served as turning points in society, as well as turning points in generational identification. Usually, the impact that these events have on society will be holistic in nature whereas the impact on the members of the generation is often based on factors such as age and location. For example, when the United States was attacked during the September 11, 2001 terrorist attack, the effects on society were different from the effect on the individual members, yet not separate. The country as a whole was thrust into a war-time era that included heightened security in all public places, most notably the controversial airport security and the threat level scales (cnn.com). The country saw an immediate increase in the government's ability to delve into their private life via newly passed laws that were intended to give law enforcement agencies the ability to track possible terrorist plots (i.e., The Patriot Act) (justice.gov). These changes are still being felt in our country to this day. Looking at the effects on members of different generations, some Gen Xers were stepping into the ensuing war as soldiers, many of whom had parents who had fought in the previous war in the Persian Gulf. On the other hand, most members of the **Millennial Generation** do not know an existence where America has not been fighting the war on terror. Millennials also do not know what could technically be known as "peacetime" in their country. Clearly, the result of the attacks on America has shaped how those who live in the country see the world around them, but each generation saw a different result. As stated earlier, every generation has specific turning points that help define who they are. The individuals in Generation X know what both peacetime and war are like, the same as the generations before them, but thus far much different than those who have come after them.

Millennial Generation Individuals who were born between 1982 and 2002.

This is not just specifically centered on politics, as everything going on in the world will have an effect. For example, where Generation X seemed shocked when cheating scandals in sports were announced, Generation Y only knows baseball in the steroid era, NBA referees betting on games, and compliance issues in the NCAA. Where members of previous generations still are angered or surprised about the growth of controversy in sports, Millennials see it as a part of sports; an unfortunate part, but the norm nonetheless.

© rvisoft/Shutterstock.com

Generational Time Frames

When people ask the question "who is generation . . .?" they are asking much more than who the individual members of the generation are. Yes, they would like to know when the generation begins and ends; however, they usually are also wanting to identify what traits are common among members of each generation, what influences helped shape each group, and what is the lasting impression these individuals have made, or are expected to make, on society. Ironically, in order to be able to answer the question holistically, the time frame that encompasses each generation is one of the most important factors of research in this area. It is also often one of the most inconsistent factors in generational research. Time frames for generational research tend to vary, usually caused by a lack of consensus as to how long each generation should last. It is not uncommon for research to set different time frames for generations that vary between 10 to 20 year spans (Howe & Strauss, 2007; Huntley, 2006; Twenge, 2006). Though creating a generational time frame for a study is often seen as a decision for the researcher to make, a well tested and therefore established theory exists that can be used for establishing consistent time frames.

Theory of Generations the need to combine both time and experiential factors was that to fully understand a generation, one needed to take both a positivistic and phenomenological approach or risk missing crucial aspects of what made one generation different from those before and after.

Theory of Generations

In an attempt to make an argument for the consistency issue in generational research and to help provide a solution to this ever-present problem, Karl Mannheim (1952) established his **Theory of Generations**, in which he acknowledged the collective nature of both time and experiences as influential in the development of generational time frames, as well as the identifiers of the different stages of the blocks which help solidify the whole of the generational block. The argument made by Mannheim for the need to combine both time and experiential factors was that to fully understand a generation, one needed to take both a positivistic and phenomenological approach or risk missing crucial aspects of what made one generation different from those before and after. Essentially, he saw the need to combine both quantitative and qualitative research methods to frame generations.

Mannheim looked to the work of philosophers David Hume and Auguste Comte to help establish an acceptable time frame for a generation to encompass (Mannheim, 1952). Hume and Comte individually looked at how an individual's life is lived from two very different viewpoints. Hume argued that both personal and shared experiences work together to create cohorts of individuals who live on a social continuum (Mannheim, 1952). Hume also argued that one cohort will learn from those who came before them while, in time, they will work to lead those who are their juniors.

Mannheim saw the importance of this phenomenological approach to generational theory, but also understood that a solid time frame for when and how generations should be grouped was equally important. For this, Mannheim looked to Comte's work for guidance in establishing a suitable time frame that would properly encompass a generation. Comte broke an individual's life down into a three significant phases: youth, adulthood, and retirement (Mannheim, 1952). According to Comte, each of these phases accounted for a 30-year span of the individual's life. From Comte's argument, Mannheim established that a generational span of 30 years would be suitable for determining who the members of a generation are, as well as what behaviors or traits can collectively be considered identifiers of each cohort. By using this positivist and phenomenological approach to combine time and experience, Mannheim's theory offered the clearest and most holistic look at any single generation to date.

Mannheim's Cohorts

As stated earlier, Mannheim (1952) looked to Hume's work on the social continuum of cohorts, or groupings of generational members, as a starting point for establishing his theory. According to Hume, individuals learn from their experiences throughout life. These experiences can be solely based on an individual's own experience, shared experiences based on societal change, or those others experience but the individual is privy to (Mannheim, 1952). Though Hume puts a lot of emphasis on learning from one's own personal experiences, he states that some of the most important lessons are learned from others, especially individuals who came before them. The example that Hume used to explain the concept of the social continuum was that of a political system where the elders guide the understanding of the youth until it is the younger generation's time to take over and lead (Mannheim, 1952). Mannheim acknowledged that, although each generation will react to their experiences based on their own perception of the events that are taking place, we all learn from our parents, teachers, family members, and the many other "elders" in our lives about how society perceives the events. This is not to imply that younger people will always believe what their elders believe in, or even agree with what they are teaching, but they will still learn from the previous generations in the end, even if it is only learning what the younger individuals do not believe in, or how they feel about or perceive events that are happening around them.

Hume's argument for how we learn about the world around us and create individual perceptions about society explained how different age cohorts comprehend the world around them, but it stopped short of explaining when individuals moved from being "youth" to being and "adult" or an "elder." This is where Mannheim again turned to Comte. Comte sought to explain the progression of an individual's life through breaking it down into the three distinct stages of one's life—youth, adulthood, and retirement years (Mannheim, 1952). Having broken these different phases into 30-year spans, Comte was able to explain how individuals are able to take time to learn, use, and later share knowledge throughout their lifetime. During the first 30 years of life, or their youth, people are being introduced to the society around them and the world at large. They are learning how to become the leaders of society from their experiences and the experiences of others. Once they hit 30 years old (assuming a clear start and stopping point for these phases), these individuals enter the second stage of their lives, adulthood, and it is time for them to take on the leadership roles in society (Mannheim, 1952). During this stage, individuals are able to utilize the information they have learned during their youth and are responsible for moving society forward. After adulthood comes an individual's retirement years, during which time one will leave his or her leadership role in society and become a teacher of the future generations. The progression of an individual from being a student of life, to a society leader, to a teacher shows how experiences are shared, as well as how the continuum progresses to keep society moving forward.

WHAT A DIFFERENCE THIRTY YEARS MAKES

As stated earlier, generations are not just about the experience, but also about the time and events that make up these experiences (Mannheim, 1952). When Mannheim turned to Comte's work on the stages of life, he found the answer he was looking for: Comte argued that generations should encompass a 30-year time span in order to coincide with three distinct stages of one's life (Mannheim, 1952). As stated previously, these three stages are: *youth*, *adulthood*, and the time of one's life that would usually constitute *retirement* years. From birth to adulthood, what Comte termed youth, is the time when people learn the lessons that they need to be productive members of society (Mannheim, 1952). Youth is a time when we learn from many different individuals such as parents, teacher, religious leaders, coaches, friends, and family (Mannheim, 1952). Each of these individuals will leave their impression on us and help us to form our own opinions on a variety of topics. Some of these individuals we will agree with and some we will not; however, it is through the interaction with these individuals that we learn about the world around us, and how we form the values and beliefs that will lead us through to the next stage in life (Mannheim, 1952).

Comte's argument that we do not enter adulthood until around the age of 30 is contradictory to the traditional belief that one becomes an adult at 18, but Comte was referring to an age when the responsibilities of society shift from one generation to the next. We see it in the workforce as promotions become more available after working in a career for a specified amount of time. As individuals progress through adulthood, they continue to shape the society around them, and in the process, shape the experiences of the younger generation. At the end of adulthood, the process of passing on the reins of power and transitioning oneself into retirement begins. In considering how Comte's time frame includes many of the same ideas that Hume outlined in the social continuum argument, we can see that the combination of the two was an easy match for Mannheim.

SOCIAL CONTINUUM IN SPORTS

Social continuums can be seen in sports when you look at most any team's legacy. For example, there are countless college football programs that are consistently in the top 25 in the college football preseason rankings, and many of these teams are contenders for a Bowl Championship Series game, the coveted season-ending game for Division I college football. This includes schools such as Ohio State University, University of Oklahoma, University of Notre Dame, University of Texas at Austin, University of Michigan, and Stanford University, to name a few. Because of the continued legacy of these teams, they often are the top picks for the best high school football players who are heading into college and looking for a chance to play for a NCAA championship. Although these teams have seen coaching staff changes, as well as player changes throughout the years, they are able to continue their success because of the social continuum that persists within these sport organizations. The history and traditions of these programs are passed down from one generation of players and coaches to the next, usually resulting in continued success for decades. Because college scholarships span 4-5 years, the "generation of players" is more fluid because of the time frame in which college athletes are in attendance.

In his explanation of the social continuum, Hume used the example of political systems to describe his social continuum and how learning can flow from the older generation down to the younger (Mannheim, 1952). Again, the argument was that this process needed to take place in order for the youth to know how to keep the political system working without having to reinvent the wheel when a new individual took over the leadership role. This is essentially what happens when a new coaching staff, or a new cohort of players, comes into a program. Some may argue that a new coaching staff will be brought in to enact change in the system, and that is true; however, the core of tradition and what the team is trying to achieve will stay the same.

Athletes are also an important part of the social continuum for sports teams. They not only share common experiences with the members of their own cohort, but they also share these experiences with the athletes that come after them. Cohorts in athletics, just like in academics, consist of the group of individuals that come in as a graduating class. Part of belonging to a generational cohort is the common experiences that those members share, and this is the same for academic and athletic cohorts. Therefore, if we apply Hume's argument about social cohorts to athletic cohorts, events that happen in and to athletic teams will affect the team in one manner, but will affect the cohort in another. For example, if a team is experiencing a losing streak, a coach may opt to bring in successful alumni to talk about tradition and past success as a motivator to the new generation of athletes. Tradition is spread from one player to another, year-to-year, and even through the images and slogans that are presented in locker rooms or athletic complexes. This is the social continuum in action.

Mannheim's Stages of Life		
Youth	**Adulthood**	**Retirement**
The time when individuals learn from the adults in their lives how to be productive members of society. These including teachers, parents, religious leaders, and coaches.	The stage where individuals take on the responsibilities and needs of the society they live in. They begin to shape the society and therefore help begin to shape the youth in the process.	Individuals leave their roles in society, passing on the responsibility to those in adulthood. They continue to mentor the youth.
Birth to 30 years of age	31–60 years of age	61 years of age to death

FROM THEORY TO APPLICATION

Seeing how much an individual did within the 30-year time frame, and seeing how researchers could identify what events could be instrumental in shaping how a cohort thinks or behaves from just one section of this time frame, Mannheim set 30-year blocks as the time format for generational cohorts. As research progressed, Mannheim's use of the 30-year time frame to investigate experiences and behaviors continued, but there were some alterations. The use of both a positivist and post-positivist approach to generational research still continues; however, the time frame is one factor that continues to change. For example, two of the top scholars in modern generational research, Strauss and Howe (1991; Howe & Strauss, 1993; 2003; 2007), have taken Mannheim's work and shorted cohorts to 20 years. Some opt for 15-year spans, and others have brought it down to 10. But overall, the theory still stands as one of promoting a mixed methodological approach to generations.

WHAT IS A MILLENNIAL?

Understanding the similarities and differences between generations can help understand how and why society has changed, or needs to change. Generational research has been used in nearly every facet of society to help people understand what the individuals in said society want. From fashion to entertainment, from parenting to education, from the workforce to retirement, everyone wants to be ready for what is next. To know this is to know generations. The Millennials have been seen as a driving force in society as a whole (Alsop, 2008; Howe & Strauss, 2003, 2007; Huntley, 2006; Twenge, 2006). From the cradle to the workplace, the Millennials are, without a doubt, changing the world around them (Alsop, 2008). Many people have been witness to this change and asked the question, "What is it about *this* generation that is making everyone take notice?" It is simple, the Millennials have power. . .and they know exactly how to use it (Alsop, 2008; Huntley, 2006; Twenge, 2006).

A "Millennial" is the pop culture label that is used to describe the generation of young people that were born between 1982 and 2002 (Howe & Strauss, 2003; Howe & Strauss, 2007; Huntley, 2006). Unlike the generation before them, they are seen as a positive and productive cohort versus the "slacker" label that was given to Generation X (1961–1981) (Howe & Strauss, 2003; Howe & Strauss, 2007; Huntley, 2006). Where Generation X seemed to take on the role of fixers for society after the end of the Vietnam War and Reagan Era economy, the Millennials,

or Generation Y, seemed to have a nearly clean slate to create the world that they would like to see. This mindset for Generation Y is ironic, as they have been witness to many events that have caused limitations to their lives. Do not tell Millennials they cannot do as they please because they will usually tell you otherwise as they have often worked past these perceived limitations to meet with success (Twenge, 2006).

The Millennials have had a very different road to travel when compared to Generation X and the Baby Boomers (Howe & Strauss, 1993). The Millennials are predominantly the children of Baby Boomers and early Generation X (Howe & Strauss, 2003; Howe & Strauss, 2007; Huntley, 2006). As Generation X was seen as a disappointment to their elders, and often portrayed as an example of what you did not want your child to turn into, it seems like society was eager not to turn out another generation of "Xers" (Howe & Strauss, 1993). Millennials were raised in a much different era of parenting than their immediate predecessors, even though they were born immediately after Gen X (Howe & Strauss, 2003; Twenge, 2006). For example, in 1982 the first "baby on board" car signs went on sale, and everything from kitchen door locks and child safety seats regulations were overhauled (Howe & Strauss, 2003; Strauss, 1993; Twenge, 2006). Parents fought hard to make sure their children were happy, and felt loved and special every day and in every activity (Howe & Strauss, 2003; Twenge, 2006). The term *trophy kids* was coined to refer to the Millennials as they were often seen getting participation awards to make sure that they did not have to deal with the disappointment of losing (Alsop, 2008; Twenge, 2006). Because these awards were often the work of parents trying to protect their children, the term *helicopter parent* is often used to describe the parent of a Millennial (Twenge, 2006).

The overprotected lives that Millennials lead can often be in stark contrast to the world that actually exists around them. This may be the cause of the helicopter parent behavior; however, that has yet to be determined. Such optimists in their everyday lives, Millennials actually have seen many ups and downs in the world around them. The oldest Millennials were in high school when they witnessed the Columbine High School shooting take the lives of members of their own generation, and they were ready to head to college when a similar event occurred at Virginia Tech University (Johnson, 2008; Twenge, 2006). These events were followed by the September 11, 2001 terror attacks, growing economic decline throughout the world, and for many, they have only known the US fighting the war on terror (Johnson, 2008; Twenge, 2006). Of course, there has also been good in society. This includes the election of President Barack Obama as the first African-American president, as well as a technological boom that has connected them with information and individuals in ways that once seemed impossible (Howe & Strauss, 2007; Twenge & Campbell, 2009; Twenge, 2006).

As parents and society have worked to protect this generation from the dangers and disappointment of the world, these others' behaviors have created an ego boost for Millennials. This has developed into what is known as the "Generation Me" mentality (Twenge, 2006). As Generation Me has been told how special they are throughout their lives, Millennials are not comfortable with the idea of criticism (Twenge, 2006). Active avoidance of criticism has led the Millennials to outwardly seek information that can help guide them in the direction to success and away from failure. Now, you might say that everyone wants to succeed, so how does this make Millennials different? The difference lies in the behavior of Generation X versus Generation Y.

As much as Generation X and their superiors, or elders, did not see eye to eye, Generation X did not often outright question what they were told to do (Howe & Strauss, 1993). Did this cohort follow every rule and command they were given? No, but they learned early on that it was easier to say "okay" and do it your own way, if necessary, rather than question (Howe & Strauss, 1993). Generation X was not afraid to make mistakes and not afraid to not be perfect as they were so often used to being seen in a negative light (Howe & Strauss, 2003; Twenge, 2006). Because Millennials seem worried about being seen as less than what society has built them up to be, or what they believe they need to be to succeed, many have not learned to work issues out without guidance at every turn, which, because of current technology and availability, they have not had to look far to find.

Though Millennials are worried about failure and disappointing others, they are not above challenging the hierarchies they work in (classroom, workplace, family) and to ask any questions needed to get the information they may need (Twenge, 2006). Twenge (2006) offers an example of this when she describes the experiences of one of her colleagues at San Diego State University. This particular professor was surprised by how unaware his students seemed to be of the traditional hierarchy by questioning their professors much more often than students in the past. His students did not see a problem with telling professors that they were wrong or pointing out mistakes the professor had made in grading because the student did not receive an A. This behavior has been noticed in many different aspects of society including, most recently, the workforce (Alsop, 2008; Sujansky & Ferri-Reed, 2009).

MILLENNIALS IN SPORTS

The question of "How do we work with Millennials?" has clearly been asked by the powers that be, and sports are no different. The leadership style in sports is often autocratic, containing assertive and aggressive communication (Rocca, Martin, & Toale, 1998; Vargas-Tonsing & Bartholomew, 2006). Most Millennials are not used to this type of communication style. On the playing field, coaches are the individuals in charge and players are expected to listen, but how well does this structure work with a generation who are accustomed to a more flat hierarchy that they have essentially created themselves?

Millennials and Power

The Millennial generation is often referred to as Generation Y or, more appropriately, "Generation Why?" because of their tendency to ask questions of anybody and everybody around them (Twenge, 2006). This behavior has led some to see the Millennials as disrespectful or even entitled (Twenge, 2006); however, this is not always the case. Yes, the argument that Millennials are an entitled generation is not unfounded; they are the trophy kids after all (Alsop, 2008; Huntley, 2006; Twenge, 2006). In order to understand the difference between the expectation for constant praise and the continuous questioning behavior you have to look at the goal of the two behaviors separately.

Not Without My Trophy

Millennials thrive on praise. This should not come as a surprise to anyone. This generation was raise to succeed and, at every turn, their parents, teachers, and, now, employers often shower them with accolades (Alsop, 2008). Trophies for participation (e.g., 8th place ribbons in track and field competitions, one for each lane in the track), and expectations of help all along the way are the norm for this generation. The old sport concept of learning in defeat or waiting for your turn to play seems foreign to many from the Millennial Generation. Evidence of this exists in college sports; there seems to be an increase in transfers for student-athletes who do not get as much play time as they expected, or feel they deserve (sportingnews.com). Some athletes will even quit a sport after a rough season rather than give it one more try. Why? Because society has made Millennials believe that anything is possible if you just try. If they do not succeed in every single aspect of life or endeavor they attempt, which was not seen as impossible or a tragedy just one generation earlier, Millennials feel as if they have failed themselves as well as the individuals in their lives (Huntley, 2006). So, how do you succeed when you are not sure how to complete the task you are facing? You ask questions, and a lot of them. Welcome to Generation Why.

© matimix/Shutterstock.com

Questions asked for information seeking is not something new by any stretch of the imagination. People have been asking questions and sharing information since as far back as history can trace. So why do we see the questions that Millennials ask as different from those that have been used to communicate in the past? Many have found fault with the content of the questions the members of this generation ask, simply because they seem like common sense (Alsop, 2008). Others have found issue with the questions asked simply because the information seems to be that which is easily gotten if the Millennials would just take time to look for it (e.g., it is in the syllabus) (Alsop, 2008; Twenge, 2006). Though these are valid concerns, these are hardly issues that would warrant discussion. The most surprising and, in sports settings, the most problematic behavior for Generation Why would be the individuals that they find it acceptable to question (Twenge, 2006). For reasons that scholars have yet to be able to explain, Millennials seem to be the first generation to ignore the structure of existing hierarchy and simply address individuals they feel could provide the answers being sought (Huntley, 2006). Beyond creating problematic situations, this behavior can often create shifts within the power dynamics that can be harmful for athletic teams if they are not understood and accounted for.

DYADIC POWER THEORY

Power defined as "the capacity to produce intended effects and, in particular, the ability to influence the behavior of another person even in the face of resistance".

In a definition compiled from a multitude of previous studies on power dynamics, the concept of **power** has been defined as "the capacity to produce intended effects and, in particular, the ability to influence the behavior of another person even in the face of resistance" (Dunbar & Abra, 2010, p.658). In sports power is structured through a team hierarchy that includes team captains, assistant coaches, head coaches, and, in professional leagues, members of the management team. A team's hierarchy is put into place as a means of managing a team, just as is the case with an organizational hierarchy. Just as responsibilities are distributed through the different roles in these team or organizational structures, so is power. **Hierarchical structures** are usually understood as a power organization where every level up the hierarchy is a level up in power. Though these structures are often easily identified, power is still a fluid entity that can move between the individuals in a conversation with or without the intent of the

Hierarchical structure organizational power structures where every level up the hierarchy is a level up in power.

Dyadic Power Theory
1. Increases in relative authority are related to increases in relative resources.
2. Increases in relative resources produce increases in relative power.
3. Increases in relative authority produce increases in relative power.
4. The relation between perceived relative power and control attempts is curvilinear such that partners who perceive their relative power as extremely high or low will make fewer control attempts, although partners who perceive their relative power as equal or nearly equal will make more control attempts.
5. An increase in the number of control attempts will produce a greater probability of an increase in the amount of control.
6. As a partner's perception of his (her) own power relative to that of his (her) partner increases, his (her) countercontrol attempts will increase.
7. Countercontrol attempts have a negative effect on control for the initiator of the original control attempt.
8. The relation between perceived relative power and satisfaction is curvilinear such that partners who perceive their relative power as extremely high or low will report lower levels of satisfaction compared to part THE JOURNAL OF FAMILY COMMUNICATION, 4(3&4), 235–248

From "Dyadic Power Theory: Constructing a Communication-Based Theory of Relational Power," The Journal of Family Communication, 4(3&4). Copyright © 2004 Lawrence Erlbaum Associates, Inc. Reprinted by permission of Taylor & Francis, Ltd, http://www.tandfonline.com

individuals in the interaction (Berger, 1994). This dynamic has been defined by Berger (1994) as "the product of interactions between people and not the result of individuals' desires to wield influence over others" (p. 458–459).

Dyadic Power Theory is a communication theory that explains just how power can shift from one individual to another in a conversation, often multiple times, without either individual intending to take or relinquish power during the exchange (Dunbar, 2004). When considering power exchanges between individuals, many different components need to be explained in order to fully understand how communication can influence these dynamics in relationships. Initially, thinking that power shifts happen only as a result of overt challenges would be a mistake. Though those do make up a portion of power exchanges, unintentional power seeking behaviors also constitute power shifts. As is implied by the name, these behaviors are not enacted purposefully, and therefore the resulting power shifts are not always noticed in the rapid pace of a conversation (Berger, 1994).

When a message is sent from one individual to another, two levels of understanding influence exist that help explain how power exists in, and influences, dyadic communication, they are *content level understanding* and *relational level understanding* (Berger, 1994). **Content level understanding** looks at the literal words being used to create messages and what these words are meant to express (Berger, 1994). **Relationship level understanding** is based on the meaning of and within the relationship at the base of the dyadic communication. When an athlete questions the instruction of his or her coach, the question can be seen

Dyadic Power Theory (DPT) a theory that explains just how power can shift from one individual to another in a conversation, often multiple times, without either individual intending to take or relinquish power during the exchange.

Content level understanding investigates the literal words being used to create messages and what these words are meant to express.

Relationship level understanding investigates the meaning of and within the relationship at the base of the dyadic communication.

in one of two ways: a question or a challenge based on the actual words used to phrase the question, and the relationship between the coach and athlete. Consider this scenario, if the coach is open to conversation and the questions of his or her athletes, the question will be just that, a question. Perhaps the athlete needs clarification or did not hear the coach's requests/comments. The question would not be perceived as a challenge to the coach's power. If the coach was not accepting of input or questions from athletes, the question asked in the same manner and with the same words as in scenario one would be perceived as a challenge to the coach's power based on the relationship at the core of the dyadic interaction.

Though context and interpersonal relationships are at the core of power issues in communication, examining power in dynamic communication is more complex than these two factors seem to make it appear. Breaking down the relationship factor further can help explain why individuals may want to challenge power as well as how these challenges may be exhibited. These relationships are also used to understand the types of power that are present between individuals. Athletes who know that this coach-athlete relationship is closed for questioning but still ask questions will be perceived as challenging and possibly problematic. Those who respect the relationship will be seen as following protocol.

In an attempt to better understand power in communication, Dunbar (2004) looked to the work of Rollins and Bahr (1976) and others to help explain how power is manifested, challenged, and subsequently relinquished and/or obtained during conversation. Dyadic Power Theory (DPT) stemmed from the growth of Rollins' and Bahr's (1976) research on power dynamics in family relationships; however, Dunbar (2004) developed DPT, allowing it to be used to assess dyadic communication in relationships outside of family settings. Dunbar (2004) broke down factors that influenced power, including: social exchange, equity, interdependence, sex roles, and relational history and control. Accordingly, the definition of power changed to encompass the expanded scope of DPT to "the ability or potential to influence or control the behavior of another person" (Dunbar, 2004, p. 238).

DPT sees one's perception of power as just that, an individual's perception, not necessarily the reality of the relationship (Dunbar, 2004; Rollins & Bahr, 1976). Perceptions of power are contingent on the individuals in the relationship (e.g., coach-athlete, captain-teammate, teammate-teammate). According to DPT, how individuals perceive power is contingent upon the perceived power of the individual they are interacting with (Dunbar, 2004). The perceived partner power is also an influence upon the control attempts that each individual may exhibit during the interaction. Control attempts are defined as "attempts by one person to change the behaviors of another" (Dunbar, 2004, p. 238). These perceptions may not reflect the reality of power differentials; however, control attempts are still related to the need an individual has to control the power in the relationship.

DPT is based on eight propositions. Proposition One proposes that "increases in relative authority are related to increases in relative resources" (Dunbar, 2004, p. 240). This proposition explains that with authority comes the ability to influence resources that are made available to others. For example, a coach has more power than a team captain. This means that the coach has more decision-making ability than the captain. So where a team captain has the authority to carry out the requests or "orders" of a coach (e.g., to run drills, get the team together for meetings, start practice), he or she does not have the power to make the orders. The coach's authority stems from his or her position as the head of the team, and the resources would be the knowledge of the sport as well as the coaching skills that he or she has.

Propositions Two and Three are predicated upon the authority and resources established in Proposition One and the influences that they have on power. Proposition Two maintains that, "increases in relative resources produce increases in relative power" (Dunbar, 2004, p. 240). Where Proposition Three states, "increases in relative authority produce increases in relative power" (Dunbar, 2004, p. 240). These propositions indicate the two most important factors in establishing relational power. Referring back to the example with the coach and the team captain, though both are seen as leaders, and both have power within the team dynamic, the coach has more power in the interpersonal dynamic. Because the coach controls the resources, and has more authority based on the team hierarchy, he or she has more relative power.

Proposition Four states that the relationship between one's perception of the power dynamic in the encounter/relationship and his or her attempts to gain control is curvilinear (Dunbar, 2004). This means that an individual who perceives that they have more power than their communication partner will be less likely to make attempts to gain power because he or she does not believe they need to take another's power. However, the proposition also states that those who perceive equal power make more attempts at control. (Dunbar, 2004). With this proposition, Dunbar (2004) moves away from Rollins' and Bahr's (1976) original argument that attempts to control power would be more evident from the high-power individual versus the low-power individual. The original assumption was that control attempts would be a result of attempts to retain power as a means of attaining one's goal (Rollins & Bahr, 1976). Proposition Four also makes the argument that goal attainment is essentially the *goal*, but takes DPT a step further than Rollins and Bahr by stating that individuals in either high or low-power positions will execute control attempts if he or she sees that being in the high-power position is necessary. So, according to DPT, coaches' behaviors will not turn to power attainment until they believe their power is equal because they believe power is necessary to do their jobs.

Proposition Five, "an increase in the numbers of control attempts will produce a greater probability of an increase in the amount of control," (Dunbar, 2004, p. 241) focuses on the probability of power shifting from one individual to another by way of a shift in communicative control (Dunbar, 2004). An example of this proposition would be an assistant coach who wants to have more input in the team's schedules or game planning. If the head coach is insistent upon retaining control, the assistant will need to continue to work to gain some of the power through repeated control attempts. If the coach eventually relinquishes some control, it would be clear that the repeated control attempts were successful. Had the assistant coach not continued, and the coach not relinquished control, the lack of control attempts would also prove the proposition correct.

Control attempts are the focus of Propositions Six and Seven. Both of these propositions explain the receiver's reaction to control attempts of his or her communication partner (Dunbar, 2004). Proposition Six states, "as a partner's perception of his or her own power relative to that of his or her partner increases, his or her contercontrol attempts will increase" (p. 242). The reaction to the control attempts will either be "accepted" in one of two ways and the receiver will allow for the control to move to the sender (i.e., the head coach will give the assistant coach some control). The alternative is that the receivers will resist the control attempts and utilize countercontrol attempts in the process (i.e., the head coach will reduce the control of an assistant coach). This is the "result" of Proposition Seven, "countercontrol attempts have a negative effect on control for the initiator of the original control attempt" (Dunbar, 2004, p. 242).

This can influence the overall satisfaction of the interaction. This is the focus of Proposition Eight, which states that perceived relative power influences levels of satisfaction. Essentially, relational partners who perceive a more equitable level of power in a relationship are more satisfied with their experience than those who perceive greater differences in relational power. This specific proposition is interesting when considering the change that Millennials are bringing to interpersonal communication. Perceived power balance in sports is often a benefit for athletes as the different types of athletic relationships usually function well when dominance is not at the center of the relational dynamic. This proposition can also help explain how coach-athlete relationships involving the Millennial Generation are able to function even when the relationship is usually based on clear power differentials.

Despite their questioning nature, and perceived disregard of hierarchy, Millennials really do respect and recognize authority. Though many individuals see the Millennial behavior of going straight to the top for answers as "jumping ranks" and ignoring hierarchy, it could also be understood as respecting the positions that are at the top as being those who are most in the know. Millennials would not seek the assistance of the powerful to help solve even the smallest of problems if they did not understand and respect the ability of those at the top of the chain of command. This generation does respect power; however, throughout their lives they have been given the perception of equality within interpersonal relationships (Huntley, 2006; Twenge, 2006) most likely creating more of a flat perception of power with individuals of authority. Basically, this generation may just be less intimidated by power because they do not see the span of power differences between themselves and authority figures, creating a positive perception of communication experiences where others who sense the positions of high and low power would not be comfortable in the interaction. Examples of these more equitable relationships in sports are more flat power structures within coaching staffs as well as team captains who serve as peer leaders within the player ranks.

Types of Power

Three power types that exist, and influence how control attempts are made, in relationships are manifest, latent, and invisible power (Dunbar, 2004; Komter, 1989). These power types are based on the relationship present as well as the goal of each individual participating in the interaction. **Manifest power** is described as power that is a result of an outward attempt by an individual in a conversation to gain control of the power in a conversation (Dunbar, 2004; Komter, 1989). Though questioning an individual, such as an athlete questioning his or her coach's orders, could be an attempt at taking power, it could also be an attempt to ask for information. This is where both the content and relational level of understanding mentioned before are crucial to investigating power within a relationship (Berger, 1994; Dunbar, 2004; Komter, 1989). As in the previous example, a coach's power could shift if they typically do not accept or answer athlete questions and yet answer this question. Understanding the content of the question/comment is important to find out what the athlete was seeking from the exchange (Berger, 1994). Because manifest power is based on the intent to take power from another, what the individuals are saying is important to find out if control attempts are being displayed, and if they are successful or not. **Latent power** describe the attempts at or techniques for conflict avoidance that someone in a less powerful role would use to avoid being perceived as challenging the power of their communication partner who is in a more powerful role (Dunbar, 2004; Komter, 1989). So an athlete not questioning their coach or finding a way to work around the question if they need to ask one would be considered latent power. **Invisible power** represents "implicit values, beliefs, or preconceptions that precede behavior" (Komter, 1989, p.207). Rather than being part of the plan for the conversation, this type of power comes to be as the conversation happens. The context and behaviors of the conversation will influence the power exchanges, therefore it is invisible as a source of actual power.

Manifest power power that is a result of an outward attempt by an individual in a conversation to gain control of the power in a conversation.

Types of Power		
Manifest	**Latent**	**Invisible**
Power that is a result of an outward attempt by an individual in a conversation to gain control of the power in a conversation.	Attempts at or techniques for conflict avoidance that someone in a less powerful role would use to avoid being perceived as challenging the power of their communication partner who is in a more powerful role.	The values, beliefs, or preconceptions that come about because of the content and context of the conversation. This type of power is less based on role before the interaction but rather the conversation itself.

WHAT THIS MEAN FOR SPORT COMMUNICATION

Relationships in sports are unique; this is not a secret to anyone, but just how unique can be seen in the differences between Millennial behavior in sports and their behavior in the rest of their lives. Where issues of power struggles have been shown in the family, education, and workplace dynamics, Millennials tend to be less aggressive in their communication in sports. Does this mean that athletes are still interested in autocratic, top down, *you will run until I am tired*, type coaches? No, they are not bipolar in their sports and the "outside" world. But they are not as interested in challenging the hierarchy in sports as they are in other areas of their lives (Johnson, 2008). In sports, as research has shown to this stage, Millennials are more interested in being heard and treated fairly than they are in overhauling the sports world.

According to (Johnson, 2008), on the playing field, Generation Y wants to be able to give input into how their team is run, but not as a means of challenging the power of the coach. These athletes are more interested in assisting as a means of making sure that they succeed at the highest level. Again, success is one of the main goals of this generation as a whole. The trophy kids really just want another trophy, and they do believe that their input is necessary to be able to achieve this end result. It makes sense, as they have been asked their preference about most aspects of their daily lives. Why not volunteer it? When they are not heard, they begin to question whether or not they are being looked out for. This behavior is one that society has taken to in most non-sports settings (as students you probably have been/will be asked to evaluate your professors at the end of the semester), so why not do so in this aspect? And this input goes beyond just what plays are working or not. The Student-Athlete Advisory Committees (SAACs) have been part of the NCAA guidelines since 1989. They are an effort to make sure that athletes have input into the rules, regulations, and policies that affect their lives (athletics.atu.edu). The negotiation of power for athletes within the team hierarchy has been rather tame compared to the non-sports realms.

This, however, does not take into account the behavior of Millennial athletes off the field or court. This is where being members of the Millennial Generation does seem to show more often. This generation of athletes does tend to accentuate the sense of entitlement that most members of their generation are known for (Huntley, 2006; Twenge, 2006). From the "one and done" college athletes to the expectation that they do not have to follow the rules because they are "famous," Millennial athletes do seem to feel that they are above the norm in some situations (Hill, 2013). Examples abound when looking to the problems that college athletics has been facing in trying to control the NCAA rule against extra benefits being given to college athletes. From Ohio State University and "Tattoo-gate" to Johnny Manziel and the infamous half-game suspension for his alleged unsanctioned autograph sessions, athletes tend to challenge the sports power structure in blatantly disobeying the rules, rather than asking and arguing for their wants.

Though college athletes tend to give the most examples of these issues, professional athletes are also known to expect more than athletes that came before them. How often have players argued that they should be allowed to renegotiate their multimillion-dollar contracts after one standout season? Or demanded trades if they are not given these contracts immediately? Team salaries have skyrocketed in this post Jerry Maguire "show me the money" world, and to what end? It often seems like the logos on the front of the jerseys are no longer as important as the name on the back. Just ask LeBron James (Hill, 2013). With lockouts looming after nearly every season, and NCAA players demanding to be paid for their playing time, power shifts in sports are taking an interesting turn as the Millennial Generation starts to dominate the playing field.

DISCUSSION QUESTIONS

1. What is the biggest differences between the Millennial Generation and Generation X?

2. How do millennial view power and how can that influence the different sport dynamics?

3. How does the perceived sense of entitlement influence collegiate athletics, consider Northwestern footballs attempt at unionization?

4. How will social media and Generation Y extended use of the multitude if platforms influence the rules and norms of athletics at the many levels of sport from youth to professional?

REFERENCES

http://athletics.atu.edu/files/saac-brochure.pdf

Alsop, R. (2008). *The trophy kids grow up: How the millennial generation is shaking up the workplace*. San Francisco, CA: Jossey-Bass.

http://www.bcsfootball.org/news/story?id=4809856

Berger, C.R. (1994). Power, dominance, and social interaction. In M.L. Knapp & G.R. Miller (Eds.), *Handbook of interpersonal communication* (2nd ed., pp. 450–507). Thousand Oaks, CA: Sage.

Dunbar, N.E. (2004). Dyadic power theory: Constructing a communication-based theory of relational power. *Journal of Family Communication, 4,* 235–248.

Dunbar, N.E. & Abra, G. (2010). Observations of dyadic power in interpersonal interaction. *Communication Monographs, 77(4),* 657–684.

Howe, N. & Strauss, B. (1993). *13th Gen: Abort, retry, ignore, fail?* Vintage Press: New York.

http://www.cnn.com/2011/POLITICS/01/26/threat.level.system.change/

http://www.justice.gov/archive/ll/highlights.htm

Howe, N. & Strauss, W. (2007). *Millennials rising: The next great generation*. New York: Vintage Books.

Howe, N. & Strauss, W. (2003). *Millennials go to college: Strategies for a new generation on campus*. Great Falls, VA: American Association of Registrars and Admissions Officers and LifeCourse Associates.

Huntley, R. (2006). *The world according to y: Inside the new adult generation*. Crows Nest, NSW: Allen & Unwin.

Johnson, G. (2008). Studying the "millennial" relationship. *The NCAA News*. p.8.

Komter, A. (1989). Hidden power in marriage. *Gender & Society, 3,* 187–216.

http://www.soonersports.com/ViewArticle.dbml?ATCLID=208806147

Rocca, K.A., Martin, M.M., & Toale, M.C. (1998). Players' perception of their coaches' immediacy, assertiveness, and responsiveness. *Communication Research Reports, 15,* 445–450.

Rollins, B.C. & Bahr, S.J. (1976). A theory of power relationships in marriage. *Journal of Marriage and the Family, 38(4),* 619–627.

Strauss, W. & Howe, N. (1991). *Generations: The history of America's future 1584 to 2069.* New York: Wiliam Morrow and Company, Inc.

Sujansky, J.G. & Ferri-Reed, J. (2009). *Keeping the millennials: Why companies are losing billions in turnover to this generation - and what to do about it.* Hoboken, NJ: John Wiley & Sons, Inc.

Twenge, J.M. (2006). *Generation me: Why today's young Americans are more confident, assertive, entitled – and more miserable then ever before.* New York: Free Press.

Twenge, J.M. & Campbell, W.K. (2009). *The narcissism epidemic: Living in the age of entitlement.* New York: Free Press.

Mehrabian, A. (1971). *Silent messages.* Belmont, CA: Wadsworth Publishing Company, Inc.

CHAPTER 5
GROUP COMMUNICATION

Chapter Objectives

At the end of this chapter, readers will be able to:

1. Distinguish between cohesion and locomotion in teamwork.

2. Explain how task cohesion and social cohesion are both crucial to team success.

3. List the three levels of individual relationships that help build social capital.

4. Give examples of how a coach's communication behavior can: 1) undermine and 2) build a team's social identity.

Key Terms

Team	Bonds	Informal role
Cohesion	Bridges	Formal role
Locomotion	Linkages	Social capital
Task cohesion	Role ambiguity	Social Identity Theory
Social cohesion	Objective ambiguity	

INTRODUCTION

Team a group of individuals working together for, or associated through, a common activity or task.

Team. This one word is used in every industry, in every country, every single day. What meaning comes to mind when that one word is used, however, will vary per industry, per country, per day. Does team equate to a group? Is a team the differentiation of a group of winners versus a group of losers? Is a team an organization? Each of these definitions, among many others, would all be correct depending on the context of the use of the word team. When individuals speak of teams, they usually are referring, in some capacity, to a group of people working towards a common goal. Teams will sometimes meet with success and sometimes with failure, but the collective effort put into a task is often the identifying factor that will indicate teamwork and the title of a team. This chapter will define what teams are based on cohesion and efficacy.

© bikeriderlondon/Shutterstock.com

HOW DOES A TEAM WORK?

Through all of these definitions of "team," one common factor that is necessary to help teams succeed is the presence, or a least the perception, of cohesion. Cohesion has been defined in Merriam-Webster dictionary as "a condition in which people or things are closely united" (merriam-webster.com). In sports, the idea of cohesion is often associated with the concept of a team working together, not much more detail is generally considered when making a statement of a team playing together. However, in the literature from both sport communication and sport psychology, the factors that make a team a "team" are more detailed. Bollen and Hoyle (1990) defined **cohesion** as "an individual's sense of belonging to a particular group and his or her feelings of morale associated with group membership in groups" (p. 482). Cohesion has been linked to team success as well as players' satisfaction with their athletic experience (Widmeyer, Carron, and Brawley, 1993).

Cohesion "an individual's sense of belonging to a particular group and his or her feelings of morale associated with group membership in groups".

THE DECISION

"I'm gonna take my talents to South Beach and, um, join the Miami Heat" (Abbott, 2010). These 14 words, spoken on an ESPN special on July 8, 2010, crushed most of Northeast Ohio and sent waves of celebration through the city of Miami, Florida. In the time it took him to utter that phrase, LeBron James changed the landscape of the National Basketball Association (NBA), or so it seemed. James' move to Miami, along with Chris Bosh, to join Dwayne Wade, seemed to have instantly created a basketball dynasty in South Beach. The news made headlines for two reasons. First, because of the spectacle that was made of the trade; there was an hour-long special on ESPN, whereas most trades are simply announced in a short press conference or a news release (Abbott, 2010). And second, because James, who was born and raised in Akron, Ohio and drafted to the Cleveland Cavaliers straight out of high school, was considered a hometown hero who had promised he would deliver a championship to a city whose last championship was with the Cleveland Browns in 1947 (espn.go.com). In 2007, Cleveland faced the San Antonio Spurs in the NBA finals, and though the Cavs were swept, the city looked to James to lead them to the finals once again (NBA.com). Instead he was leaving his team, and his home, to win a championship for Miami.

The day after what became known as "The Decision" was made, James was in Miami for a welcome reception that could only be rivaled by championship celebrations. The city came out in full force, and the event, which was televised once again by ESPN, kicked off with Wade, Bosh, and James elevating from below center stage like rock stars coming out during a concert. The trio were dubbed the "Three Kings" by Eric Reed, Heat announcer, and the crowd roared with excitement as the players came down a runway amid smoke and lights,

© meunierd/Shutterstock.com

giving high fives to the fans at floor level (Blinebury, 2010). During the on-stage question and answer session with the three players, James promised the city that the Heat would win multiple rings for fans in his now infamous, "not one, not two, not three . . ." quote (Blinebury, 2010). Everyone was ready for next season.

ONE YEAR LATER . . .

Fast-forward to the following May. The Heat finished the season with a 58-24 record tallying 11 more wins than the team had posted the year before, made quick work of their playoff opponents, and were in the NBA finals facing the Dallas Mavericks (nba.com). The 2011 NBA Finals drew some of the highest viewership since the 2000 series between the Los Angeles Lakers and the Indiana Pacers (nba.com). Considering not many people gave Dallas a chance against the "Big Three" (as their nickname had transitioned), most people were watching the Heat, who had become a polarizing team since their launch party. Be it to fail or succeed, the Heat were the draw of that series. The Mavericks had another storyline planned for NBA fans. From May 31 to June 12, Dallas led Miami down the path to failure and humiliation. They played like a team on a mission, like a team out to prove that they were not the underdogs, like a team who were a *team*.

After the six-game series was over, the Big Three walked off the court looking dejected and as if they were still searching for something that would prove to be their biggest issue throughout the rest of their tenure together. For the next three years the Heat would struggle with the one thing their opponents would capitalize on, their lack of cohesion as a unit, and not just a three-man show. James, Wade, and Bosh would lead the Heat to the finals every year from 2011 to 2014, even winning back-to-back titles in 2012 and 2013, but during those series, the only team who did not test them was the young Oklahoma City Thunder team (who would not return to the finals again).

Other than the Thunder and the Mavericks, the only other team the Heat would face would be the San Antonio Spurs (nba.com). In 2013, the seven-game series would go down as one of the best in Finals history, complete with a controversial game six and nail-bitter game seven leaving fans feeling like they had just witnessed history, something truly special (Harper, 2014; Martin, 2013). The Spurs were touted as a group of old men who were well past their prime, and the Heat were seen as the new era of superstar basketball. The Heat prevailed in 2013 and were expected to do the same in 2014; however, something interesting happened . . . cohesion, or as many would call it, teamwork.

COHESION

The concept of group dynamics was first named and conceptualized by Kurt Lewin (1935), who was on the forefront of leadership studies. Lewin (1935) defined two principal aspects that create the concept of a group. First is cohesion with the second being locomotion. With **locomotion**, the group is exhibiting the behaviors that are needed to achieve their objectives (Lewin, 1935). Cohesion describes how the group comes together, works together, and maintains the relational aspects of a group to help keep the group working (locomotion). Bringing teams together to create the necessary locomotion is often very difficult, as many teams have found out.

Locomotion: an instance where the group is exhibiting the behaviors that are needed to achieve their objectives.

Not One, Not Two...

When the Miami Heat lost to the Dallas Mavericks, many pointed to the fact that the Mavs had played together as a team for several years, where the Heat had only played together for one year with the current starting five at the helm. Though teams change players every year, many believe that longevity with a line up can add an advantage to the team, which will lead to success. These assumptions are not necessarily wrong. The longer a team plays together, the greater the opportunity for teammates to get to know and understand each other. The assumption would be that this would allow for cohesion to develop; however, developing cohesion is not as simple as that.

A second definition of cohesion from Merriam-Webster defines the term as "the act of sticking together tightly" (www.merriam-webster.com). This is the most basic definition of the complex concept that is cohesion in sports. Within the realm of sport cohesion that there are two levels of cohesion that can influence both whether or not a team has a winning season, as well as if an athlete choses to return for another season of play (Turman, 2003; Widmeyer, Carron, & Brawley, 1993).

Yukelson, Weinberg, and Jackson (1984) point to Festinger, Schachter, and Back's (1950) definition of cohesion to explain how cohesion influences inter-group dynamics. They found that cohesion includes attractiveness of group membership as well as group goal achievement. These two factors can break down into what we now identify as social and task cohesion. Using this defi-nition as a guide for their study, Yukelson et al. (1984) found that the college basketball teams in their study perceived cohesion as focused on "common goals, valued roles, teamwork that is complementary to the goals that the group is striving to achieve, and interpersonal attraction or attraction to the group itself" (p. 112). This shows clear examples of both *task cohesion* (roles, goals, and teamwork) and *social cohesion* (attraction). It is also clear that, though some of these factors may have more influence than others depending on the season and the needs of the team, both task and social cohesion are crucial to team success. For example, if a team is on its way to an undefeated season, the group will likely focus on both task and social cohesion equally. They would want to keep the winning streak intact for the potential of achieving a championship (task), and would also likely work to keep the perfect season because it is some-thing that they have all worked for together and not something that many ath-letes and teams can experience (social).

Where this is an example of both types of cohesion working together, a team who may not be finding success might only focus on the social cohesion of working to improve and strive together through adversity.

Task Cohesion

Of the three types of cohesion men-tioned, the focus on team goals comes from the development of task cohesion. **Task cohesion** has been described as the members of a team coming together for the completion of a given task (Carron, Widmeyer, & Brawley, 1985). Essen-

tially, task cohesion means that a team will come together for the sole purpose of meeting a given goal (Horn, et al., 2012). This level of cohesion describes the most basic level of group work; however, in sports, this is crucial to team success.

For all levels of sport, goals are essential to team planning. Goals provide both teams and individuals with the opportunity to outline behaviors and mile-stones they need to accomplish in order to achieve their goal. Basically, in a reverse manner, goals provide the tasks that teams need to be committed to in order to work towards success. For these tasks to be reached, teams need to

Task cohesion de-scribed as the mem-bers of a team coming together for the comple-tion of a given task.

© Kjetil Kolbjornsrud/Shutterstock.com

come together as a unit to find the most effective and efficient way to complete each task. This is task cohesion.

The process of a task as a means for bringing individuals together is not a new phenomenon. Nor is this a concept unique to sports. Take a look at the popular series *The Walking Dead*, for example; the whole concept of the show centers around strangers, many of whom would never have spoken to each other before, working together to keep each other alive. The characters can be seen risking their lives for individuals they know little more about than you may know about the classmate sitting next to you. It is the ultimate goal of being alive at the end of the day, and hopefully the next morning on through the possible end of the zombie apocalypse, that brings these groups of people together. That is their task, and they all know they need the help of others to achieve it. Though most groups do not have as dramatic of a goal as those in *The Walking Dead*, the focus of a goal is still a powerful motivator. This example how a common task can generate into a cohesive relationship between individuals is obvious, but with this characters on the show, there also exists a social aspect to their relationship.

Task Cohesion and Individual Roles

Part of working in a group includes understanding the job, a task, which the group has to complete. At the basis of breaking down the task into accomplishable parts is understanding who is responsible for each aspect of the task (Eys & Carron, 2001). A lack of understanding in these roles creates what Eys & Carron (2001) described as **role ambiguity**. Much like the differences in other areas of sport research, role ambiguity in sport also differs in how the concept is applied in analysis. Because the hierarchy within a sports team is much smaller than most organizations, so the opportunities for ambiguity to arise are fewer. However, when it does arise, because it is a rare occurrence, it can also be more difficult to deal with (Bass, 1980; Eys & Carron, 2001).

Usually within groups, a leader is the individual who generally identifies what each individual needs to do to help the group. In sports, the person in charge is usually a coach who is expected to communicate these responsibilities to the players. However, just because a coach, or any leader, gives instructions does not mean that everyone understands what was told to them. The two types of ambiguity that center around this level of task completion are objective ambiguity and subjective ambiguity (Eys & Carron, 2001).

Objective vs Subjective Ambiguity

Objective ambiguity describes the lack of certainty an individual has about his or her responsibilities based on factors stemming from the environment or his or her physical state (Eys & Carron, 2001; Khan et al., 1964). So, for example, if a coach is on a recruiting trip and has to give spring training instructions to his or her team via email to an assistant coach (third party), the information may not be clear, and due to a lack of ability to ask questions, may not be

Role ambiguity a lack of knowledge or understanding as to what their role is in the group, usually associated with the group task.

Objective ambiguity the lack of certainty an individual has about his or her responsibilities based on factors stemming from the environment or his or her physical state.

understood completely. Though the role of the assistant coach is to relay the message, there is always the opportunity that the message will be stated in a manner that is different from how the head coach might have said it; therefore, it may not be understood by all in the same manner, which creates subjective ambiguity.

Where objective ambiguity is focused on the lack of understanding on behalf of the team, subjective ambiguity is based on the personal perception of the athlete. (Eys & Carron, 2001) With **subjective ambiguity**, the information has been delivered to the player by the coach, but the player does not perceive that they have all the information he or she needs. He or she may believe they understand all the details, but believe that they simply do not understand what was told to them. An alternative would also be that the athlete believes he or she does understand the instructions, but in actuality, what he or she understood, their interpretation of the message, was incorrect. This could be anything from a wrongly executed play call to running the wrong drill in practice, to missing a team meeting because the athlete misunderstood a meeting time.

Subjective ambiguity the information has been delivered to the player by the coach, but the player does not perceive that they have all the information he or she needs.

The connection between objective and subjective ambiguity relates to the aspect of sport cohesion on a deeper level than just the understanding of a specific task. The ambiguity that results from the above-mentioned circumstances has as much to do with understanding the actual words spoken as it does with the understanding of each individual in the relationship. If a coach and a player, or even a player and player, have a strong enough relational dynamic, their ability to understand each other increases. Thus, subjective ambiguity decreases as cohesion increases. This can be demonstrated in the nonverbal communication that takes place when coaches call in plays by use of hand signals, or even in the famous "stare" of legendary Tennessee women's basketball coach Pat Summitt that let everyone know something was not right. When ambiguity exists, and team members are not able to carry out their responsibilities, the team is not able to achieve the goals that the group has set forth for themselves (Eys & Carron, 2001).

Types of Role Ambiguity	
Objective Ambiguity	The lack of certainty an individual has about his or her responsibilities based on factors stemming from the environment or his or her physical state.
Subjective Ambiguity	An individual receives information, but he or she does not feel as if they have enough to fully understand their role.

The roles that individuals have set for them are considered **formal roles** and delineate the behaviors that each individual is responsible for based on the task set forth and are intended to maximize team potential (Bray, 1998; Eys & Carron, 2001). This is critical to the success of a sports team, as each position

Formal role group roles and behaviors that each individual is responsible for based on the task set forth and are intended to maximize group potential.

Informal role group roles that are not specifically defined nor assigned.

has different assignments in each play and on the team as a whole. By contrast, **informal roles** are not specifically defined nor assigned. These are usually roles such as de facto leaders, or team "cheerleaders" intended to raise the energy level or morale of the team (Eys & Carron, 2001). The coach does not usually select these individuals; rather they come about organically based on the level of cohesion that has been established with the team, as well as the leadership ability of the individual.

Once the members of the team are able to fully understand what their own role is they are able to better execute within the team dynamic. Essentially, if all individuals know exactly what they are expected to do, they will also able to understand the roles that their teammates are expected to fulfill, and what they are able to expect from their teammates. This allows teams to function as a unit, towards the execution of their goals. If, and when, the team understands the roles and task breakdown, they are able to work towards the task cohesion mentioned in the beginning of the chapter. The clarity of the role and the task cohesion developed work towards team cohesion. Within sports, team cohesion and social cohesion are both equally important factors.

Social Cohesion

Social cohesion defined as a team coming together to serve a social function.

Social cohesion has been defined as a team coming together to serve a social function (Carron et al., 1985). The different factions that surface during the progression of the show *The Walking Dead* are great examples of how social cohesion works. These groups are not only formed as a means of physical (living versus dying) survival, they are also used as a means of maintaining the emotional and mental health of the characters. The groups are meant to help form a sense of identity and to help fulfill the socialization needs of every individual. Abraham Maslow (1943), in his Hierarchy of Needs, listed "love and belonging" needs just above the physiological and safety and security needs. The satisfaction of these third-level needs is present in the story lines of *The Walking Dead*. When the character of Carol kills members of her group to keep a

© Helga Esteb/Shutterstock.com

disease from spreading, the group leader, Rick, decides that Carol broke the social rules of the team and banishes her with food, water, and a car to get around and live in. The removal of others for safety and emotional support was her punishment. Later, when Carol works to save the group from others who are trying to kill them, she does so to regain Rick's trust and with the hopes of returning to the group again. Carol's return, though at that point she knew she could survive on her own, show the social support a group is able to provide to an individual.

According to the Organization for Economic Co-operation and Development (OECD) publication on social cohesion (2011), cohesion is developed on social capital, social mobility, and social inclusion (oecd.com, 2011). All of these factors can be traced to the example of the groups in the show *The Walking Dead* used in the example above, but they can also be used to trace the sense of cohesion in sports. Team members need to rely on their teammates to help them grow as individuals and as a group. Without your teammates, it is difficult to build success, however it may be measured for that team. When looking to each factor listed above, it is easy to see how all three lead back to a sense of togetherness within the group. **Social capital** looks to what each member can bring to the team and their teammates individually.

The OECD describes social capital as having three separate factors that can explain how individuals relate to others and what those others can bring to a relationship in the form of social capital ("What is social capital?," n.d.). These are bonds, bridges, and linkages. **Bonds** are described as links that people have with their family, friends, and/or culture based on the perception of a shared sense of identity. **Bridges** are those who are considered acquaintances such colleagues, associates, or distant friends. They are meaningful individuals in a person's life, but are not so close as to share a common sense of identity ("What is social capital?," n.d.). Finally, **linkages** are less than acquaintances, so even further removed from the source and less likely than the other two to provide social capital for the source. Teams and teammates would, hopefully, fall under the bonds and bridges categories as they would need to be close enough to share a sense of common identity to drive individuals to share goals and to develop task cohesion.

> **Social capital** identifies what each member can contribute to the group and the other group members individually.
>
> **Bonds** described as links that people have with their family, friends, and/or culture based on the perception of a shared sense of identity.
>
> **Bridges** individuals who are considered acquaintances such colleagues, associates, or distant friends.
>
> **Linkages** individuals who are less than acquaintances, so even further removed from the source and less likely than the other two to provide social capital for the source.

Social Cohesion

Being a member of a group is usually associated with a positive sense of self and self-identity (Haslam, 2004). Abraham Maslow (1943), in his new famous Maslow's Hierarchy of Needs, listed as love and belonging needs just above the needs of food, nourishment, and shelter. Because we have this need to be "part of something," we often feel this sense of common ability in working towards something bigger or better than what we perceive can be achieved alone as motivating, because we do not want to let our team down (Eys, Hardy, Conon & Beauchamp, 2003). This particular sense of task cohesion is closely related to the concept of social cohesion.

Being a member of a task-based team, such as is the case in sports, has proven to have a strong correlation to a process of social identity (De Backer et al., 2011). In their study focusing on team identification and cohesion, De Backer & colleagues found that, within the group of elite athletes they investigated, group identity was often allowed to prevail over

their person identity when necessary. Essentially the athletes allowed their own status as an elite athlete to take a back seat to what was needed for the team to succeed. This sense of team identity is often a function of the social cohesion that is experienced by individual athletes when they are part of a team.

As teams continue to develop bonds set forth through task cohesion, the bonds between their individuals often became increasingly stronger. Individuals begin to identify as members of the team versus individuals who are playing on a team. Haslam's (2004) **Social Identity Approach** has been used to explain how this transition takes place (De Backer et al., 2011). Haslam's approach combines individual aspects of both Tajfel's (1972) Social Identity Theory as well as Haslam's own concepts covering personal identity. **Social Identity Theory** describes how individuals can more internally identify with the group than with outsiders of the group (Tajfel, 1972). Under this theory, the individual's sense of self is interlocked with the sense of the group. The best example of this sense of group and team identity is shown in the movie *Miracle* (O'Connor & Guggenheim, 2004). When Herb Brooks, coach of the Team USA Hockey for the 1980 Winter Olympics, selected the top players from the collegiate ranks as a means to bring a championship team together, many of these young men were currently playing for teams who saw themselves as college rivals. They had fully "bought in" to the long-standing traditions from their respective universities and made them their own; therefore, the rivalries outweighed the allegiance to the national team. The players had already experienced Tajfel's theory at one level, and now they were expected to shed these identities to be able to play for their country. Through training camps, games, and some fights between teammates, the players were transformed into a team and finally able to find their identity as Team USA. At that point, the team realized they were better by being 100% invested in their goal than by trying to play as individuals (O'Connor & Guggenheim, 2004).

Haslam (2004) would describe the need for the members of Team USA to keep their current identity under his self-categorization theory as one's sense of unique self identity (Haslam, 2004). Though the team members saw themselves as members of their college teams, and therefore had a team identity, this team identity was still an outsider's identity from the current insider groups of Team USA, so it was therefore still unique.

As is evident from the Team USA example, relationships between teammates are crucial to the development of a sense of team cohesion, both in the task and social cohesion aspects. This makes sense if you consider you would not want to associate your identity along with someone you do not like, or want to be like. Likewise, if teammates cannot get along, getting everyone to work for the same task is extremely difficult. As stated in the beginning of the chapter, even professional sports teams like the Miami Heat need cohesion to function at a top level. Communication between individuals is the cornerstone of the development of immediacy between teammates and immediacy is an important part of cohesion.

As discussed in Chapter 2, immediacy, or a sense of liking, is a contributing factor to the sense of satisfaction and success within a team (Martens & Peterson, 1971). Martens' and Peterson's (1971) research identified a "circular

Social Identity Theory describes how individuals can more internally identify with the group than with outsiders of the group.

relationship between satisfaction, cohesiveness, and success" (p. 58). According to Widmeyer, Carron, & Brawley (1993), 83% of sports-based research suggests a positive correlation between cohesion and team success based on research between members of successful teams compared to members of losing teams. This would make sense, as the positive emotional arousal stemming from success can be a motivator for athletes to complete a season and continue to maintain success and attain the team goals they have set.

Working together as a group and the understanding of roles also influences the sense of the ability of the team members as well as the collective agency of the team as a whole. With the stronger sense of cohesion in a group comes members working together. This also means that separately, they will not perceive themselves as being as strong. "A group's attainments are the product not only of shared knowledge and skills of its different members, but also of the interactive, coordinative, and synergistic dynamics of their transaction" (Bandura, 1975, p. 75). This creates a strong bond between members of the team and brings a higher possibility of success, which obviously benefits the team as a whole. However, this can also cause problems if something threatens the group dynamic, such as injury. Because of the belief that the team is only as good as the sum of its parts, without all of its parts, that belief could be damaged. This is often where social cohesion can be relied upon to benefit the team. Social cohesion can help the team refocus on supporting each other and coming together for the greater cause (e.g., dedicating the season to the injured teammate).

Coaches' Role

Coaches can influence cohesion by either cultivating an atmosphere of equity or difference. Whether he or she realizes it or not, the manner in which a coach treats each and every athlete can determine how well the athletes all come together (Martens & Peterson, 1971). When a coach interacts with an individual athlete, he or she may see it as a one-on-one interaction; however, when it happens in front of the other players, the interaction could mean much more. If a coach shows favoritism towards a player, even though the other players know it is not the athlete's fault, the team tends to alienate the "coach's favorite." Because the team needs to work as a team, one individual being treated differently can cause waves in the flow of the group. The same can be said for the player who is seen as the coach's least favorite (Martens & Peterson, 1971). Because the athletes do not want to be associated with the "troublemaker" or be caught in the coach's crossfire, they will usually try to stay away from the player. If the player is alienated, they do not have the opportunity to become part of the team. If they are not part of the team, there is a missing link to cohesion (Turman, 2003). It is that simple . . . but not really.

There are behaviors that can fall just short of favoritism or alienation that coaches can still show which will allow for athletes to receive praise or discipline without posing a risk to team cohesion.

If a coach praises an athlete for specific reasons, the other athletes usually will appreciate the attention paid to their teammate (Turman, 2003). The key to this coaching behavior is equity in attention so as to not cause one individual to appear to be seen as being positioned higher or lower than another on a team. Two types of behavior of both coaches and athletes that can help build cohesion are teasing and sarcasm (Turman, 2003). Essentially, what Turman found was that joking and keeping a sense of levity to practice and meetings helped keep the sport a game. Just as picking on an individual can cause a loss of respect, joking can help develop camaraderie. Keeping up a lighter side can help athletes do the same.

Beyond the behaviors of the team members themselves, outside factors can help bring a team together, as well. Beyond goals for particular season (e.g., wining record, championships, etc.), the environment can also impact how a team communicates, as well as what that communication centers around. For example, Turman (2003) found that opponents and, more specifically, the quality of these opponents, can influence how focused and how hard a team works. The goal of beating a bigger, stronger, or just overall better, opponent can influence the level of cohesion week to week.

How often has the following scenario played out in a football rivalry game: Team A is having an undefeated season heading into rivalry week and Team B has one or two wins on the season. Everyone expects a blowout victory by Team A, but Team B plays the game as if it is the NCAA National Championship game. Even if Team B does not pull off the big win, the game ends up being substantially closer than expected. When asked about the effort of the team, usually the coaches and members of Team B will point to the team coming together because of the rivalry. Teams often state that, no matter what happens during the season, you have to beat your rival. On the campus of the University of Oklahoma, for instance, you can be guaranteed to find memorabilia with "Beat Texas" on it. From shirts to caps, the presence of the rivalry game is usually present on all campuses.

WHAT THIS MEANS FOR SPORT COMMUNICATION

The presence of cohesion within the team dynamic is crucial to team success. A team, by its nature, requires all individuals to work together to achieve a common goal, which is the purest definition of success. This definition coincides with the definition of cohesion presented in the beginning of the chapter. So, it is natural to connect the need for team cohesion to the outcome of team success. Though there has been shown to be a causal relationship between the two in many studies it is possible for there to have been a few teams who were able to win as a team without either a sense of task or social cohesion present. The dependence upon factors such as role identity to form task cohesion is simply too important to goal achievement. If these teams exist, you would be hard pressed to find them, because even if the team was not bought together through immediacy or efficacy, meaning they did not particularly like each other or help each other grow, they did work together to achieve the task of winning. This means they achieved the most basic foundation of cohesion.

DISCUSSION QUESTIONS

1. What do you perceive has been the role of cohesion in group sport settings in your experience?

2. How does cohesion help, or a lack of cohesion hinder, overall team performance?

3. In your experience, which aspects of cohesion development have the biggest impact on group success?

4. In terms of role ambiguity, how can the understanding, or lack there of, of one's roles hurt team cohesion? How can it help bring out leadership opportunities on teams?

REFERENCES

Abbott, H. (2010, July 9). LeBron James' decision: The transcript. *espn.com.* Retrieved from http://espn.go.com/blog/truehoop/post/_/id/17853/lebron-james-decision-the-transcript.

Bandura, A. (2000). Exercise of human agency through collective efficacy. *Current Directions in Psychological Science, 9(3),* 75–78.

Bass, B.M. (1980). Team productivity and individual member competence. *Small Group Behavior, 11,* 431–504.

Blinebury, F. (2010, July 10). Heat go bold in presenting three kings to the world. *nba.com.* Retrieved from http://www.nba.com/2010/news/features/fran_blinebury/07/10/heat.celebration/index.html.

Bollen, K.A., & Hoyle, R.H. (1990). Perceived cohesion: A conceptual and empirical examination. *Social Forces, 69,* 479–504.

Bray, S.R. (1998). *Role efficacy within interdependent teams: Measurement development and tests of theory.* Unpublished doctoral dissertation, University of Waterloo, Waterloo, Ontario, Canada.

Carron, A.V., Widmeyer, W.N., & Brawley, L.R. (1985). The development of an instrument to assess cohesion in sport teams: The group environment questionnaire. *Journal of Sport Psychology, 7,* 244–266.

De Backer, M., Boen, F., Ceux, T., De Cuyper, B., Høigaard, R., Callens, F., Fransen, K., & Broek, G. (2011). Do perceived justice and need support of the coach predict team identification and cohesion? Testing their relative importance among top volleyball and handball players in Belgium and Norway. *Psychology of Sport and Exercise, 12,* 192–201.

Eys, M.A., & Carron, A.V. (2001). Role ambiguity, task cohesion, and task self-efficacy. *Small Group Research, 32,* 356–373.

Eys, M.A., Hardy, J., Carron, A.V., & Beauchamp, M.R. (2003). The relationship between task cohesion and competitive state anxiety. *Journal of Sport and Exercise Psychology, 25,* 66–76.

Harper, Z. (2014, March 6). Looking back: The Heat and Spurs gave us an all-time NBA finals. *CBS Sports.* Retrieved from http://www.cbssports.com/nba/eye-on-basketball/24470578/looking-back-the-heat-and-spurs-gave-us-an-all-time-nba-finals.

Haslam, S.A. (2001). *Psychology in organizations: The social identity approach.* Thousand Oaks, CA: Sage Publications.

Horn, T.S., Byrd, M., Martin, E., & Young, C. (2012). Perceived motivational climate and team cohesion in adolescent athletes. *Sport Science Review, 21 (3–4),* 25–48.

Khan, R.L., Wolfe, D.M., Quinn, R.P., Snock, J.D., & Rosenthal, R.A. (1964). *Organizational stress: Studies in role conflict and ambiguity.* New York: John Wiley.

Lewin, K. (1935). *A dynamic theory of personality.* New York: McGraw-Hill.

Martens, R., & Peterson, J. (1971). Group cohesiveness as a determinate of success and member satisfaction in team performance. *International Review of Sport Sociology, 6,* 49–61.

Martin, J. (2013, June 19). Ranking Miami Heat-San Antonio Spurs epic game 6 with best NBA finals games ever. *Bleacher Report.* http://bleacherreport.com/articles/1678814-ranking-miami-heat-san-antonio-spurs-epic-game-6-with-best-nba-finals-games-ever.

Maslow, A. (1943). A theory of human motivation. *Psychological Review, 50,* 370–396.

O'Connor, G. (Director), & Guggenheim, E. (Writer). (2004). *Miracle.* United States: Disney.

Tajfel, H. (1978). *Differentiation between social groups.* New York: Academic Press, Inc.

Turman, P.D. (2003). Coaches and cohesion: The impact of coaching techniques on team cohesion in the small group sport setting. *Journal of Sport Behavior, 26,* 86–104.

What is social capital? *The Organization for Economic Co-operation and Development.* Retrieved from http://www.oecd.org/insights/37966934.pdf.

Widmeyer, W.N., Carron, A.V., & Brawley, L.R. (1993). Group cohesion in sport and exercise. *Handbook of Research on Sport Psychology, 5,* 672–679.

Yukelson, D., Weinberg, R., & Jackson, A. (1984). A multidimensional group cohesion instrument for intercollegiate basketball teams. *Journal of Sport Psychology, 6,* 103–117.

CHAPTER 6

LEADERSHIP

Chapter Objectives

At the end of this chapter, readers will be able to:

1. Explain how leadership is a behavior, rather than a position.

2. Differentiate between values and beliefs.

3. Define autocratic and democratic leadership styles.

4. List Likert's four systems of leadership.

5. Explain why a team can be a good example of a participative leadership system.

6. Explain why coaches need to have a good understanding of different leadership roles and their advantages and disadvantages in different situations.

Key Terms

Leadership	Beliefs	Democratic leadership style
Persuasion	Likert's four systems of	Active leader
Attitude	leadership	Passive leader
Values	Autocratic leadership style	

INTRODUCTION

Leadership the behaviors of an individual responsible for guiding another individual or a group of individuals; the behaviors of a leader.

What is a leader? This may seem like a typical question that would be asked at the beginning of chapter on **leadership**, and . . . quite frankly, it is. But the question itself holds merit as it is not an easy question to answer. Not because it is such an extraordinarily deep topic that it cannot warrant one treatment in order to be answered. Rather because it is a fluid concept that constantly needs to be reassessed, even after an answer has been generated. Leadership is situational and stylistically different based on several factors that generate the different needs in each and every situation (Dainton & Zelley, 2011). According to Kotter (1990), leadership is not a position held in a hierarchy, it is a behavior exhibited by an individual. How many of you have had coaches or team captains whom you preferred over others? We often prefer these individuals based on their behavior and not just wins and losses. An(other) cinematic example of leadership preference in sports is seen in the movie *Varsity Blues* (Laiter, Robbins, Tollin, & Robbins, 1999). The setting of the movie is West Canaan High School in the fictional town of West Canaan, Texas. When the movie begins we are introduced to members of Coach Bud Kilmer's (played by Jon Voight) Coyotes, the team that is looking to bring West Canaan its record 23rd Division Championship in Kilmer's 35th year as head coach. In the tradition of Texas high school football, the town is enamored with the winning head coach and the team that gives them something to cheer about every Friday night (Laiter et al., 1999).

As the movie moves from the high school pep rally to the game that evening, it is made very clear to the movie audience that the season rests on the able arm of the town hero, starting quarterback Lance Harbor (played by the late Paul Walker). Sitting on the bench is Harbor's backup and best friend, John Moxon. Moxon (James Van Der Beek), we quickly find out does not like to play football but rather only plays for the Coyotes because it is expected, and is more than happy to sit back and let Lance take the glory. Family histories run deep with the football team and the Moxon family is no different.

Besides winning championships for the Coyotes, another tradition that has passed from father to son is the hatred of Coach Kilmer. Despite his questionable leadership techniques, the coach is still revered by the community because of his winning tradition. Additionally, though the fathers complain about the way they were treated by Kilmer when they were playing, they still support the team and pressure their sons to play because of the glory it brings to the family and the town (Laiter et al., 1999). When Lance gets hurt in the first game of the season, Moxon has to step in to lead the team. Instantly Moxon takes on the role of anti-hero in the movie as he has to manage the pressure of becoming a star and a leader without selling out to the football god complex he has so despised all his life. Moxon never wanted to lead, and he sure never wanted to play football for West Canaan, not more than sitting the bench at least. Because of this dyadic conflict of needing to be a leader while not wanting to, it becomes evident exactly how different leadership styles are often required from one individual to another for an organization to be successful (Kotter, 1990). How different leadership styles can be utilized in sport settings creates unique opportunities for conversation and research as *leaders* in sports are not always coaches or captains; they are just as likely to be the player at the end of the bench who provides support for those on the court. Because of this, "what is a leader?" is a rather appropriate question to ask.

IMPORTANCE OF LEADERSHIP

Asking about or referring to the importance of leadership may seem like an odd topic, as it is clear that leader importance is rather inherent to move any group forward, regardless of the specific setting. Though this assumption would be correct, the use of the correct style of leadership is more to the point of the discussion, as the correct style of leadership is even more important than the presence of a leader in general. In the movie *Remember the Titans*, viewers are introduced to the story of the T.C. Williams High School football team and their struggles during the Supreme Court-ordered integration of the public school during the 1971–1972 school year (Bruckheimer, Oman, & Yakin, 2000). Because Alexandria, VA was not shielded from the racial tensions that were being felt throughout the rest of the country at the time, the tensions felt by the players on the football team ran far deeper than the usual fear felt during football tryouts of not performing well and losing a starting position to a new teammate. As Coach Herman Boone (Denzel Washington) and defensive coordinator Coach Bill Yoast (Will Patton) work to establish themselves as coaching leaders for the newly formed Titans, they also encounter the task of attempting to bring the African-American and Caucasian players together as one cohesive unit.

This challenge came to a head during their summer training camp when the players' resistance to change resulted in multiple fights, a lack of cohesion, and an unwillingness to execute the plays that the coaches were trying to implement. The turning point came when the team's two most respected players, one African-American and one Caucasian, had a verbal confrontation during required player interviews. Each young man perceived, and as a result accused, the other of not working hard enough on the field and therefore not requiring other players to work hard enough. Julius Campbell, one of the top players on the defense and a leader for the African-American players on the team, confronts Gerry Bertier, another defensive player, the team captain, and a leader for the Caucasian players, about his lack of leadership skills.

Bertier:	Listen, I'm Gerry, you're Julius. Let's just get some particulars and get this over with, all right?
Campbell:	Particulars?
Bertier:	Yeah.
Campbell:	No matter what I tell you, you ain't gonna never know nothing about me.
Bertier:	Hey, listen, I ain't running any more of these three-a-days, okay?
Campbell:	Well, what I've got to say, you really don't wanna hear 'cuz honesty ain't too high upon your people priorities, right?

Bertier: Honesty? You want honesty? Alright, honestly, I think you're nothing. Nothing but a pure waste of God-given talent. You don't listen to nobody, man! Not even Doc or Boone! Shiver push on the line every time and you blow right past 'em! Push 'em, pull 'em, do something! You can't run over everybody in this league, and every time you do you leave one of your teammates hanging out to dry. Me in particular!

Campbell: Why should I give a hoot about you, huh? Or anyone else out there? You wanna talk about a waste, you're the captain, right?

Bertier: Right.

Campbell: Captain supposed to be the leader, right?

Bertier: Right.

Campbell: You got a job?

Bertier: I've got a job.

Campbell: You been doing your job?

Bertier: I've been doing my job.

Campbell: Then why don't you tell your white buddies to block for Rev better? 'Cuz they have not blocked for him worth a blood nickel, and you know it! Nobody plays. Yourself included. I'm supposed to wear myself out for the team?! What team?! No, no, what I'm gonna do is, I'm gonna look out for myself and I'm gonna get mine.

Bertier: See man, that's the worst attitude I ever heard.

Campbell: Attitude reflects leadership, captain. (Bruckheimer, et al., 2000).

Campbell points out that Bertier is not doing anything as the team captain to fix the racial divide that is tearing his team apart, arguing that leadership is more than just giving orders, it is about demonstrating through behavior on and off the field.

Though this is a fictional representation of what really happened at T.C. Williams during their first season as an integrated campus, it is an ideal example of one of the key aspects of leadership in communication and that is persuasion. In sports, the ability to get individuals to follow a leader is achieved only through compelling those athletes to believe that the leader knows what to do, and believing that he or she is on the right path completes any type of leader. This can only be done through the use of persuasion within the communication process.

PERSUASION

Leaders often evolve from change in an environment and are required to help others create goals that are in line with the new needs of the group or organization (Dainton & Zelley, 2011). Along with the creation of these goals, leaders need to encourage people to realize those goals, as well as provide guidance and motivation for those individuals they are leading (Dainton & Zelley, 2011). This is where persuasion becomes an integral aspect of leadership communication. **Persuasion** has been defined as "a conscious attempt by one individual to change the attitudes, beliefs, or behavior of another individual or group of individuals through the transmission of some message" (Bettinghaus & Cody, 1987, p.7). The essence of persuasion is the understanding that both attitudes and behavior go hand in hand (Stiff, 1994). Essentially, an individual, unless being coerced, will usually not behave in a manner that is contradictory to the attitude he or she holds on the issue at hand. So, if an individual believes that doing charitable work is important, he or she will most likely donate time or funds to a charitable organization if they are able to do so. One who does not see charity as beneficial to society is less likely to sign up to donate time or money to a charity. In sports, a high school coach who see academics taking precedence over athletics will usually excuse student-athletes from practice if the individual is having a hard time in class sooner than a coach who see both sports and school as equal. Of course, situations are rarely so cut and dried, simply because many factors can influence attitude (e.g.. the player having trouble in class could be the star and therefore both coaches would value tutoring time for practice time), but these examples create a basic understanding from which to build.

VALUES AND BELIEFS

In order to understand the relationship between attitudes and behaviors, and their influence in persuasion, it is first necessary to identify the factors that comprise "attitude." Gathering from the writings of Rokeach (1968), **attitude** is defined as "a relatively enduring organization of beliefs around an object or situation predisposing one to respond in some preferential manner" (p. 112). How and why individuals hold certain attitudes are generally connected to the values and beliefs that the same individual holds (Rokeach, 1968; Schwartz & Bilsky, 1987). **Values** are "desirable end states or behaviors that transcend specific situations, guide selection or evaluation of behavior and events, and are ordered by relative importance" (Schwartz & Bilsky, 1987, p. 551). Essentially, they are the ideals used to help make the decisions, big or small, that come up in daily life. For example, assume an athlete is trying to make a decision as to which sport to focus on for his or her senior year; he or she will look to determine which factors are most important to him or her when considering his or her participation. These would include factors such as personal and/or team success, future prospects for college play and/or scholarships, and overall enjoyment derived from sport

Persuasion a purposeful attempt by an individual or group of individuals to influence or change the attitude or behaviors of another or others through communication.

Attitude a set of beliefs that focus on a specific topic, situation, or object, which can cause a individual to respond in a partisan manner when the attitude is addressed or challenged.

Values ideals used to help make decisions, big or small, that manifest in specific communication or behaviors when address; are often ordered by importance to the individual.

© Gustavo Frazao/Shutterstock.com

participation. Depending on the athlete's values, each of these variables will help determine which sport the individual chooses to continue playing.

Beliefs influence attitudes and make up the other factor of influences on an individual's ability to resist or succumb to persuasion. Where values rely on ideals that we would like to strive to live by, **beliefs** are "a single predisposition about an object or situation" (Stiff, 1994). Beliefs allow us to judge if something is good or bad, or right or wrong. Beliefs work as an individual's moral compass, intending to help dictate the behaviors that we seek to execute. Part of being an effective leader is the ability to persuade individuals to act; to translate their values and beliefs into specific, intended behaviors. Without this ability, proper leadership will not exist.

Beliefs trust or faith in a certain person, idea, or object that one holds important; helps determine future behaviors based on a predisposition of what is right or wrong, or good or bad.

HISTORY OF LEADERSHIP IN SPORTS

When some of the greatest teams in sport history are talked about the main focus is usually the athletes that come to mind. Greatest players in baseball . . . Willie Mays, Babe Ruth, Mickey Mantle, Roberto Clemente, Jackie Robinson, Nolan Ryan, Derek Jeter (and let's face it, most of the Yankees throughout the years); Basketball . . . Kareem Abdul-Jabbar, Michael Jordan, David Robinson, Magic Johnson. These lists obviously can go on forever, but the thing that often makes this list most significant is the leaders on the list and the coaches with whom they led. When you think of Jackie Robinson you think of Branch Rickey. When you think of Michael Jordan you have to think of Phil Jackson. Joe Torre will always be connected to the name Derek Jeter, just like Gregg Popovich will be linked to David Robinson and now Tim Duncan. But just as these lists span different decades, sports, and sporting environments, they also encompass the spectrum of leadership styles that each of these players and coaches represent. So what exactly are "leadership styles"?

LEADERSHIP STYLES

AUTOCRATIC AND DEMOCRATIC LEADERS

When originally identifying the two primary leadership styles, Lewin and Lippitt (1938) determined the difference between autocratic leaders and democratic leaders was based on the role that the leader took within the group as well as the resulting group dynamic that developed. The study was originally intended to find out how social group trends develop among students in elementary school. The groups of students in the study were given the task of creating a mask with materials that were evenly supplied to each group. Once the task was initiated, the researchers observed how the dynamic developed between each group of students as a result of determining members' duties, including who surfaced as the leader of the group (Lewin & Lippitt, 1938). Though the intent of the study was simply to observe social interaction, the end result was the initial identification of democratic and autocratic leadership traits.

Characteristics of **autocratic leaders** include demonstrating more of a leader focused communication style and *focusing* more on task completion than on the needs and skills of the group membership (Lewin & Lippitt, 1938). These leaders used their role, and the ensuing power that the role generates, to determine which member should complete each task, and then dictate said responsibility to the individual, without seeking input from the group as to abilities and needs of each member. A general disconnect from the group dynamic carried over into the leader's lack of engagement with the members of the group. Autocratic leaders usually give orders one time and expect their subordinates to immediately follow, which proves problematic, as they usually do not offer follow-up assistance during the task completion process (Lewin & Lippitt, 1938). This style of communication tends to demotivate group members as it discredits the input that members could supply if interactions were allowed to take place with the group and leader as a whole (Eagly, Johanneson-Schmidt, & VanEngen, 2003; Lewin & Lippitt, 1938).

For democratic leaders, Lewin and Lippitt (1938) found that these individuals did utilize the power presented via the leadership role; however, rather than possess sole power in the group, **democratic leaders** tend to share power with their group members, allowing input as to how to best complete the task, and then directing and assisting throughout task completion (Eagly, et al., 2003; Lewin & Lippitt, 1938). This style of leadership not only tends to help facilitate faster task completion, but also to create a higher quality end product (Eagly, et al., 2003; Lewin & Lippitt, 1938). Where autocratic leaders look only to task completion, democratic leaders are equally concerned with group moral and individual member needs from inception to completion.

Autocratic	Demonstrating more of a leader focused communication style and *focusing* more on task completion than on the needs and skills of the group membership.
Democratic	To share power with their group members, allowing input as to how to best complete the task, and then directing and assisting throughout task completion.
Transactional	• Residing between the typical democratic leader and the laissez-faire style of leadership. • Goals of transactional leaders include working to reward subordinates who consistently produce solid performances in their duties. • Leaders generally endorsed the reward for work method when motivating their subordinates, essentially waiting for the final product before rewarding the group for their efforts.

(continued)

Transformational	• Leaders were seen as providing a more stimulating environment for group members to work in.
	• Leaders are visionaries offering power to each group member while still managing to maintain the control necessary to lead.
	• They work with the input from their subordinates as a means for enacting change.

Bill Bowerman

Assertive coaches are anything but an anomaly in sports (Rocca, Martin, & Toale, 1998; Vargas-Tonsing & Bartholomew, 2006). Though this is not necessarily the preference of current athletes (Turman & Schrodt, 2004), the yelling, angry, sideline pacing, autocratic coaches are not quite extinct as of the writing of this book. One example of this coaching style many individuals are familiar with is the University of California, Los Angeles' John Wooden, aka The Wizard of Westwood (Roy, Greenburg, & Bernstein, 2008). Wooden had his athletes trained to run like a machine running each drill right down to the second in practice, and it showed in their game performances (Roy et al., 2008). His team holds records such as 10 NCAA National Championships, 7 consecutive NCAA Championships between 1967 and 1973, 88 straight wins between 1971 and 1973, and 8 perfect seasons in the PAC 8 (currently the PAC 10) (Jamison, nd). Individually, any of these records would help make the argument that Wooden's autocratic style of communication is worth replicating. However, even though Wooden is known for re-teaching every one of his Bruin players how to put on their socks and tie their shoes at the beginning of each season, there is one coach who has not received as widespread attention as Wooden, but is equally as worthy of noting in this chapter. That man is Coach Bill Bowerman.

Known to most as the co-founder of Nike, Inc., Bill Bowerman was first and foremost a track coach (Moore, 2006). From 1948 to 1973, Bowerman was the head coach for the University of Oregon Ducks and translated his autocratic leadership into success on the track. He saw the need to dictate most aspects of his athletes' lives, both on and off the field (Moore, 2006). This control was sought as Bowerman believed that every aspect of a runner's life influenced the race, so why should the coach not concern him or herself all of the factors that could garner success or risk failure? For example, if an athlete were having trouble with personal relationships, Coach would give advice. If an athlete needed money, Coach would help them find a job. When he was running for the Ducks, Moore (2006) was having trouble bringing his time down in his event and, like most athletes, decided that the answer to his problem was to train more than the team-required practice time. When he found out that Moore was doing this, Bill, as he preferred to be called by his athletes, told him that rest was a better solution and demanded that the young man stop running for a while. When attempting to challenge his coach's orders, Moore told Bill that he could sit him out in practice, but could not keep an eye on him 24/7. Bowerman informed the young man that he could, easily, as everyone in Eugene knew who his runners were, and there would always be eyes on roads. Knowing that Bowerman was revered in the community, and not wanting to risk losing his scholarship by defying his coach, Moore rested. The result was as Bill predicted. Moore posted his fastest time in his next race and never doubted his coach again (Moore, 2006).

The stories of Bowerman's behavior off the field, much like those about Coach Wooden, are where the real **autocratic leadership style** is evident. Every coach is able to dictate the everyday routine of his or her athletes to an extent (e.g., practice times, days off, leaving their personal lives off the court), but not every coach can dictate even the smallest details of an athlete's lives as much as these two men did. Where Wooden changed the way the Bruins wore their socks and tied their shoes, Bowerman decided to change the shoes . . . and shirt . . . and shorts (Moore, 2006). And we are all the better for it.

To say Bowerman knew his athletes inside and out is an understatement. Bill took his knowledge of running to another level when at Oregon; and took his power to a level beyond that. In an attempt to help his athletes take precious seconds off of their time, he forced them to take themselves out of their comfort zones and work to make that the new norm. How is this different from other coaches? Bowerman did not ask his athletes if they were willing to do more, he only asked for their input after it all was done. He usually relied on the positive results to persuade his athletes that he was right and reduce the negative affect associated with the changes (Moore, 2006). For example, when he realized that athletes could run in thinner material in order to reduce wind resistance and the weight that cotton retained when collecting sweat throughout the duration of a race, Bowerman decided to reinvent his runners' uniforms. The athletes complained that they felt naked on the course while running; however, they stopped complaining when their times started to drop as a result (Moore, 2006). When Bowerman wanted to reduce the weight of the athletes' shoes in order to again cut time, he ordered that each athlete have a shoe made by the staff to fit each foot perfectly, left and right sized separately. Though this resulted in higher costs for equipment and extra time spent by the staff to build the shoes, the result was a better time and, eventually, Nike running shoes.

Some may say that Bowerman was simply looking after his athletes and being a good and attentive coach, and they would not be wrong. However, in this case, with this coach and John Wooden alike, the power that the coach wielded and the lack of autonomy on behalf of the athletes to have a say in how the team was managed, would fall under autocratic leadership. Bowerman, like Wooden, micromanaged as much of the team, and as was told by Moore (2006), as much of the athletes' personal lives as was possible all in the name of team success. Though the autocratic style bred champions, it was extreme, especially considering the time frame in which each of these coaches was gaining the most success out of their programs.

Both Wooden and Bowerman coached during rather turbulent times in American culture. As these men were growing their programs to be strictly guided and structured, America was losing control of the same youth that these coaches were able to keep tight reins on (Moore, 2006; Roy et al., 2008). When campus protests, long hair, and anti-establishment movements were taking over universities throughout the nation, the rules of the Ducks and the Bruins, to name the teams written about here, were considered sacred by the athletes

Autocratic leadership style demonstration of more of a leader focused communication style and focusing more on task completion than the growth of the group members in the process.

who represented them. This trend is not uncommon through the ages, though some of the control that coaches have traditionally had in the past has lessened (Rocca, Martin, & Toale, 1998, Vargas-Tonsing & Bartholomew, 2006). Coaches have always been afforded more control by their players, and usually under one specific condition . . . that the athletes understand that the coach has the athletes' best interests at heart (Rocca et al., 1998; Turman & Schrodt, 2004).

PROGRESSION OF LEADERSHIP

As leadership research progressed the dynamic between autocratic and democratic leadership started to become more in depth, and as often happens when similarities and differences become pronounced, so do the alternatives. Other leadership styles, such the very hands-off style of the laissez-faire, began emerging, leading to the eventual identification of the transactional and transformational leaders (Bass, 1985; Bass, Avolio & Atwater, 1996; Eagly, et al., 2003; Kruger, Rowold, Borgmann, Stanfenbiel, & Heinitz, 2011). Pulling together the information from the more recent studies created a picture depicting the evolution of leaders from autocratic to laissez-faire and those that fit in between. The most dynamic of these are the transactional and transformational leadership styles defined in Chapter 1.

LIKERT'S FOUR SYSTEMS OF LEADERSHIP

In the example from the movie *Varsity Blues* in the beginning of the chapter, John Moxon was forced to step into the leader role when Lance Harbor got injured. He had to lead the team to finish the game, and after that to finish the season as district champions. Prior to that moment, Moxon was never seen by anyone, friends, family, or teammates, as anything but a backup to Lance. However, when he was able to put together a winning drive to finish that first game, he became a perceived by all as a leader. His team, and the town, started to see him as someone whom they could count on to lead their team to the district championship. He became a leader.

Likert's four systems of leadership the system argues for the progression of leadership styles as needed to keep up with changes in the organization or group.

The progression of leadership has been outlined in **Likert's four systems of leadership** (1961). In this theory, Likert argued that as time brings change to an organization, or in this case a team, leaders need to continue to change as the times require change. Though change is never as easy to implement at an organizational level, as the evolution would require either behavioral change or a personnel change to take place, on a sports team the transition can be a little smoother as change is more common. For example, when coaches are not successful over multiple seasons, they are usually terminated and a new coach comes in to lead the team. Another example of change is simply when players change teams, because the player moves to a new location, school, or even grade. Change is expected in sports settings. Because of this, new leaders often emerge when situations call for them to happen; one player or another will usually step up into the role of leader to help keep/get their teammates on the right track.

Likert (1961) identified four systems within his theory covering the characteristics of the four different types of leaders explained by the theory. **System 1** identifies leaders that are similar to authoritative leaders from the work of Lewin and Lippitt (1938) in that the leaders use a top down approach for information flow. These leaders dictate all their orders down to their subordinates who, in turn, do not have an avenue for input into the goals and methods for reaching these goals. These leaders use fear and threats as a means to gain power and control over their subordinates and to have them simply follow the instructions given to them. The subordinates under these types of leaders are often hostile, as they do not feel empowered in their positions, and as a result, usually display a lack of overall satisfaction in their jobs (Likert, 1961).

To once again use *Varsity Blues* as an example, as the season progresses, Moxon's distrust of Coach Kilmer and distaste for his leadership methods leads to a predicament for the coach, which in turn leads to a moral dilemma for the quarterback. Before becoming the starting QB at West Canaan, Moxon's future was focused on an academic scholarship to Brown University, which he finds out he has earned the week before the division championship game. Unlike most of his teammates, Moxon's ticket out of West Canaan was never football, and his coach knows this. When Moxon does not become the submissive subordinate that Coach Kilmer is used to, Kilmer threatens to falsify Moxon's transcripts to lower his GPA, which will result in the revocation of the full scholarship to Brown. This use of threats and fear make Kilmer the perfect example of a System 1 leader, often referred to as an *exploitative authoritative leader* (Dainton & Zelley, 2011; Laiter et al., 1999; Likert, 1961).

What is common in most System 1 leader-led organizations is a general lack of production and a higher than normal turnover rate among subordinates. In sports, this usually happens at the pre-collegiate levels, because of the ease at which these early level athletes can leave and re-enter the sporting realm if they do not like their situation. If you do not like your team or coach there are other clubs or schools to play for before you get to the college level. In college and beyond, NCAA transfer guidelines, the scarcity of scholarships and open positions in college sports, and later even less opportunity to make a professional team can make moving from team to team even more difficult. Though leaving a pre-collegiate level sport team is easier, coaches/leaders in middle and high school athletics would not often suffer as high of a turnover rate with this style of leadership.

System 2, also called the *benevolent authoritative system*, still utilizes the top-down communication method; however, leaders are more strategic in their communication style (Likert, 1961). They offer employees an opportunity to contribute to the decision-making process; however, only on items the management allows them to have input on. Management in this system uses both offers of rewards as well as threats of punishment as employee motivators. The rewards are used as an incentive to get members to buy into their programs or ideas, where the punishment is an avoidance technique (Dainton & Zelley, 2011).

This is more common to the sports realm as rewards and threats are often used as motivators at all levels. Rewards of easier practices or a day off can be used for positive performances in games, where threats of more difficult practices or being dismissed from the team are threats for poor performances or negative behavior. Coaches may ask for athlete input during game situations because the athletes may know something that is going on out on the field or the court that the coach may be missing. However, especially at the high school levels and below, the coach generally will still set out the team plans and goals for the games.

In the **third system,** or the *consultative system*, leaders are not autocratic in style as in the other two systems. Rewards are used more often than punishment in this system, and it is characterized by more involvement of employees in goal setting and their input is used in organizational decision-making (Dainton & Zelley, 2011). Leaders engage in conversations with employees to find out what is going well and what can be improved upon; following these discussions, they are better able to set goals. Research has found that, when given the opportunity, subordinates feel empowered through the ability to make decisions that directly involve their work environments (Dainton & Zelley, 2011; Likert, 1961). Employees are generally more satisfied and productive which helps reduce turnover.

The **fourth** and final system, often referred to as the *participative system* (Likert, 1961), incorporates participation from all employees in an organization. In this system, everyone, from managers to lower-level employees, can have a degree of input into the overall organizational goals (Likert, 1961). The participative system uses incentives to get all members to be motivated to achieve goals. Incentives can be both monetary and a perceived valued role in the organizational process. This system is believed to bring out the most production for the overall organization and results in the least turnover of all four systems (Likert, 1961). Professional sports are usually a good example of this as leaders at all levels usually can play a significant role in the outcome of the team performance. Everyone from players to trainers to coaching staff, as well as the general managers, will work together to field the best teams and create the most production to help the organization win a championship.

TRANSACTIONAL VS. TRANSFORMATIONAL LEADERSHIP

According to Bass (1997), just as was argued by Likert before him, new leadership styles emerge as organizational needs change and require different leaders to emerge. Through continued research in leadership, more styles have surfaced. Transactional and transformation leadership are the focus of more recent research on leadership communication.

Autocratic To Transformational

The coaching styles of John Wooden and Bill Bowerman did work wonders during the tenure of each of these legendary coaches, the careers of stars such as Lew Alcindor (now Kareem Abdul-Jabbar), Bill Walton, and Steve Prefontaine are just glimpses of the ability of these coaches to coach talent to another level. Though John Wooden was proud of the accomplishments of each of his championship teams, the statistics that he has stated that he was especially proud of were those that he personally kept track of, how many of his former students became professionals in fields other than professional sports (Roy et al., 2008).

Each of Wooden's former athletes still called him "coach," evidence of the success and respect this autocratic leader was able to build in his personal relationship with each athlete. As successful as Wooden and Bowerman clearly were, research suggests that autocratic leadership is not what today's athletes are seeking in their sports experience (Roy et al., 2008).

Transformational Leaders

In contrast to the transactional leader, transformational leaders were seen as providing a more stimulating environment for group members to work in (Bass, 1985; Bass et al., 1996; Kruger et al., 2011). Bass et al. (1996) described transformational leaders as visionaries offering power to each group member while still managing to maintain the control necessary to lead. Transformational leaders work with the input from their subordinates as a means for enacting change (Bass, 1985). The control and input that transformational leaders use to create structure within their group would lead some to want to categorize these leaders as autocratic; however, their mentoring of new group members and responsibility-sharing behaviors pull this categorization more towards the democratic style (Eagly, et al., 2003). Essentially, the goal is to use the input as a means to help *transform* the organization to help fit the needs of the individuals within. These leaders were often described as considerate, charismatic, inspiring, and motivational, and working to promote ethical standards (Dainton & Zelley, 2011).

Transformational leaders work to facilitate positive attitudes in subordinates towards each other and towards the organization itself, referred to as *idealized* influence (Bass, 1985). According to Eagly and colleagues (2003), transformational leaders were able to generate a sense of optimism within the group that the goal was attainable through soliciting feedback from the group members that helped facilitate problem-solving techniques when needed. This balancing act is what prompted the need for a new categorization and what makes transformational leaders unique in and of themselves.

Transformational and Transactional Leadership

Transformational leadership is one of two alternatives to Lewin & Lippitt's (1938) autocratic and **democratic leadership styles** with the other being transactional leadership (Bass, 1985; Bass et al., 1996; Eagly, et al., 2003; Kruger et al., 2011). Transformational leaders are as described as charismatic, motivational, focused on the needs on the members of the group, inspirational, as well as intellectually stimulating (Bass, 1985; Bass et al., 1996; Kruger et al., 2011). This type of leader tends to be more democratic in overall leadership; however, the leader tends to hold more power as a leader than the typical democratic leader (Bass et al., 1996).

Transactional leaders also share power with the members of the group they are in charge of, yet they often give up more power than democratic leaders, leaning more towards the laissez-faire style of leadership than the democratic style (Bass et al., 1996; Kruger et al., 2011). Transactional leaders usually focus on the end result when considering task completion and praise subordinates when the final product is produced; however, the leadership between the start

Democratic leadership style demonstration of a leader sharing power with the group members, including direction and input, as a means to assist in task completion.

Active leader individuals take time to monitor group members through the entirety of the task completion process, working towards member support and success as the project/task comes to completion.

Passive leader individuals tend to take more of a hand-off approach to guiding group members and group tasks; more incline to engage through final outcome assessment.

and the finish often varies with these leaders (Bass et al., 1996; Kruger et al., 2011). Within this leadership style, there are two different types of leaders that can surface: active and passive (Bass et al., 1996; Kruger et al., 2011). **Active leaders** take the time to monitor the group members throughout the process, working to make sure that the group members are successful and have support as they are working through the project (Bass et al., 1996; Kruger et al., 2011). **Passive leaders** are more laissez-faire in that they wait until the end of the project to find out if there are any issues with the final product (Bass et al., 1996; Kruger et al., 2011). Not only is this style of leadership not productive, but it is also bad for morale because the members do not feel appreciated when they work, nor do they feel as if they have support when problems arise (Bass et al., 1996; Kruger et al., 2011).

Transactional Leaders

Transactional leaders have often been described as residing between the typical democratic leader and the laissez-faire style of leadership (Bass et al., 1996; Kruger et al., 2011). Bass (1985) described the goals of transactional leaders as working to reward subordinates who consistently produce solid performances in their duties. These leaders generally endorsed the reward for work method when motivating their subordinates, essentially waiting for the final product before rewarding the group for their efforts. Though the reward was more democratic in style, waiting for the end result versus setting periodic milestones for rewards is reflective of the laissez-faire leader (Bass et al., 1996; Kruger et al., 2011). Three primary characteristics of transactional leaders include, first working with their subordinates to develop specific and clear objectives along with the reward for those objectives, as stated before (Bass, 1985). The second characteristic falls in line with the first in that it identifies the exchange of rewards to subordinates for the efforts given towards the identified goals. The third characteristic describes the interest of the leader in the well-being of their employees. Leaders look to the immediate needs of the workers to make sure that all their needs are met while they are working to achieve the shared organizational goal (Bass, 1985).

Though attention to group success does vary depending on the membership of the group itself, *active* versus *passive* monitoring can influence the overall success of the activity at hand. Active management of the group saw leaders who would seek out each member to determine if each individual was on task and having his or her needs meet. Though this micromanagement of the members of the group would resemble the lack of autonomy that would usually be related to an autocratic leader, the concern for the needs of the membership is a trend towards the democratic. The main concern for active managers is completing the goal set for the group, which though not a negative aspect of the style, could lead to a lack of efficacy on behalf of the group members if not implemented correctly. Just like leadership in general, the individual in charge would need to make sure that they balance an appropriate amount of task focus and member focus to make sure one does not outweigh the impact of the other.

Passive management has a stronger lean towards the hands-off approach that comes with the laissez-faire leadership style (Bass, 1997; Kruger et al., 2011). Passive managers usually did not address issues until they saw that the problems equated to a problem in reaching the end goal (Bass, 1997; Kruger et al., 2011). Though individuals may not appreciate micromanagers, the negative impact on morale was worse when problems that could have been addressed earlier were the root of failure at the end (Eagly, et al., 2003).

WHAT DOES THIS MEAN IN SPORTS?

Through the years, coaches have used many of these different leadership techniques as a means of guiding their programs and teams through their seasons. However, which leadership style is best suited for coaching truly is a question for the team and situation that each is in at the different stages of program development. Though this may seem like a means to not deciding on which style is more or less beneficial, the following will explain how and why coaches from the past and those coming up in the future need only to understand the different leadership styles to help them determine which will be best for their team in any situation that may develop. This, of course, is not a way of saying that a coach can or should transition between each style on a whim, as that could hurt the team more than help them. It is simply an explanation of how each has worked in the past with a hope to provide guidance in the future.

WHAT THIS MEANS IN SPORT COMMUNICATION

What a leader is and what a leader does are not contexts that are to be considered one and the same. As is evident in the research about the ever-changing landscape of sports, and of leadership in communication studies and beyond, "leader" is an ever-fluid concept. What needs to be understood is that leaders tend to emerge out of situations rather than assignments. Though this does not mean that the need for assigned leaders is an antiquated practice, but rather it means that the need for individuals to identify the skills of leaders, as well as the practices, is as important as ever. With multiple avenues for success available to those who are appointed to leadership roles, knowing which styles are not only more natural for the individual, but also could bring more success to the team or organization is invaluable in a sports setting.

DISCUSSION QUESTIONS

1. Which of Likert's four stages is best for which type of athletics?
2. How should a coach approach persuasion per athlete? Per team as a whole? Both?
3. Are transactional or transformational leaders better than Likert's leader? What makes this determination?
4. What environments are best for active leader or passive leaders respectively?

REFERENCES

Bass, B.M. (1985). *Leadership and performance beyond expectations.* New York: The Free Press.

Bass, B.M., Avolio, B.J., & Atwater, L. (1996). The transformational and transactional leadership of men and women. *Applied Psychology: An International Review, 45(1),* 5–34.

Bass, B.M. (1997). Does the transactional-transformational leadership paradigm transcend organizational and national boundaries? *American Psychologist, 52(2),* 130–139.

Bettinghaus, E.P., & Cody, M.J. (1987). *Persuasive communication.* New York: Holt, Rinehart & Winston.

Bruckheimer, J., & Oman, C. (Producers), & Yakin, B. (Director). (2000). *Remember the Titans* [Motion Picture]. United States: Buena Vista Pictures.

Dainton, M., & Zelley, E.D. (2011). *Applying communication theory for professional life: A practical introduction (2nd).* Los Angeles: Sage.

Eagly, A.H., Johannesen-Schmidt, M.C., & Van Engen, M.L. (2003). Transformational, transactional, and laissez-faire leadership styles: A meta-analysis comparing women and men. *Psychology Bulletin, 129,* 569–591.

Jamison, S. (nd). *The joy of the journey.* Retrieved from http://www.coachwooden.com/index2.html.

Kotter, J.P. (1990). What leaders really do. *Harvard Business Review, 68,* 103–111.

Kruger, C., Rowold, J., Borgmann, L., Staufenbiel, K., & Heinitz, K. (2011). The discriminant validity of transformational and transactional leadership. *Journal of Personnel Psychology, 10(2),* 49–60.

Laiter, T., Robbins, B., Tollin, M. (Producers), & Robbins, B. (Director). (1999). *Varsity Blues* [Motion Picture]. United States: Paramount Pictures.

Lewin, K. & Lippitt, R. (1938). An experimental approach to the study of autocracy and democracy: A preliminary note. *Sociometry, 1,* 292–300.

Likert, R. (1961). *New Patterns of Management.* New York: McGraw-Hill.

Moore, K. (2006). *Bowerman and the men of Oregon: The story of Oregon's legendary coach and Nike's cofounder.* USA: Rodale.

Rocca, K.A., Martin, M.M., & Toale, M.C. (1998). Players' perception of their coaches' immediacy, assertiveness, and responsiveness. *Communication Research Reports, 15,* 445–450.

Rokeach, M. (1968). *Beliefs, attitudes and values: A theory of organization and change.* San Francisco: Jossey-Bass.

Roy, G., Greenburg, R., & Bernstein, R. (2008). *The UCLA dynasty* [Documentary]. United States: HBO Studios.

Stiff, J.B. (1994) *Persuasive communication.* New York: Guilford Press.

Turman, P.D. & Schrodt, P. (2004). New avenues for instructional communication research: Relationships among coaches' leadership behaviors and athletes' affective learning. *Communication Research Reports, 21,* 130–143.

Vargas-Tonsing, T.M. & Bartholomew, J.B. (2006). An exploratory study of the effects of pregame speeches on team efficacy beliefs. *Journal of Applied Social Psychology, 36,* 918–933.

CHAPTER 7

FANDOM

Chapter Objectives

At the end of this chapter, readers will be able to:

1. Explain the social origins of fandom.
2. List two social benefits of fandom.
3. List the three components of group identity.
4. Give an example of nonverbal communication in fandom.

Key Terms

Imagined collective	Interpersonal communication	Collective effervescence
Group identification/group identity	Intergroup communication	Totem
	Symbol	

INTRODUCTION

As mentioned before, everyone has a central need to belong to a group (Tejfel, 1978). This should not come as a surprise to many, just consider the first thing middle and high school students do when they receive their schedules during the summer . . . they look to find out when they have lunch. This is not because teenagers love food more than anything. Though food is important, it is because they want to find out if they have lunch with their friends. They do not want to eat alone, both because it is just not fun, but also because we know there is social stigma attached to eating alone. No one wants to seem like they do not have a group of friends.

"I BLEED . . . WE ARE . . ."

Why does society have this social stigma about being alone? And why do we have such a need to belong, that when we do not belong to a group, it can

influence how we feel about ourselves? Though many have researched and worked to answer these questions, a simple response to those questions could be found in the work of Abraham Maslow (1943). According to the Hierarchy of Needs, one's sense of love and belonging sits directly above the need for safety and security, and lies directly below the need for self-esteem. So essentially, once we feel safe, we look to others in share experiences with. This also shows support for the argument that group identity helps with one's sense of self-worth translating to one's self-esteem needs being fulfilled.

SPORTS FANDOM

WHAT IS A FAN?

To understand what fandom is, it is important to first understand what a fan is. When one identifies oneself as a fan, what exactly does that mean? According to the Merriam-Webster dictionary, the definition of "fan" is "an enthusiastic devotee (as of a sport or a performing art) usually as a spectator," or "an ardent admirer or enthusiast (as of a celebrity or a pursuit)" (www.merriam-webster. com). There are a couple of interesting factors at play in these definitions. The first is the specific mention of sports in the first definition separate from celebrity, which is the focus of the second definition. This accentuates that the individual can be a fan of the sport separate from the individuals who participate in the sport. According to Reysen and Branscombe (2010), and as discussed in Chapter 1, *fanship* is defined as a connection to a team and *fandom* is one's connection to other fans of the same team. Individuals become fans of a team or an individual for many different reasons. Many of those reasons will be discussed below, but what this fandom adds to the individual's life is what draws research to the study of fandom. First, it is necessary to find out why we initially become fans of sports, athletes, or teams.

Fans of Individuals

There are a variety of reasons why individuals become fans of a specific sport. These reasons, which can be linked to fandom of either a team or an individual, include family influence, region where the individual lives, or major events (Rosenberg, 2015). For example, after the explosion of excitement generated by the 1999 FIFA Women's World Cup, there was an increase of interest by young girls in playing soccer as well as the opportunity to develop a professional league in the United States (Rosenberg, 2015). Before winning the World Cup, the US Women's National Team had a small but loyal fan following; however, during the build up to the event including clinics, advertising, and the promotions for the tournament being held in the United States, the team saw a substantial increase in attention. This led to an increase in ticket sales and, as the tournament progressed and the national team continued to win and advance, continuous sell-outs including a record crowd at the Rose Bowl in Pasadena as the US beat China in penalty kicks to win the team's second-ever World Cup (www.ussoccer.com).

© Digital Media Pro/Shutterstock.com

Sports fandom generated from becoming or being a fan of a particular athlete is often seen in individual sports, obviously, but it can happen in team sports, as well. Individual sports such as golf, tennis, swimming, or even boxing and mixed martial arts would be sports where individual athlete fandom would be present. Though individual fandom is often housed in the sports identified above, it is not uncommon for superstars to flourish in the team setting transcending the popularity of team they play for. For example, one does not have to be a fan of the Cleveland Cavaliers to be a fan of LeBron James, just like many individuals were fans of Michael Jordan even though they were not fans of the Chicago Bulls. When Derek Jeter was playing his final season of baseball in 2014, it was very common for the Yankee away games to be sold-out and

© David W. Leindecker/Shutterstock.com

for the opposing team fans to give Jeter a standing ovation as a show of respect and fandom, even if they were not Yankee fans (Castellano, 2014; Schilken, 2014). Usually, when these athletes move from team to team, their fans will follow.

Fans of Teams

Though being a fan of a sport celebrity may draw fans to one team or another, there are other factors that influence why individuals become fans of a particular sports team or teams. One reason could be due to the region where the individual is living. For example, if an individual moves to New York City for work or school, they may become New York Yankee or Mets fan. Well, unless they moved there from Boston, that is. This does not necessarily mean they will change their allegiance away from a team they may have cheered for before, but supporting the local team whose games he or she may be able to attend more regularly will help them become part of the location they now live. It can give opportunities to become part of the sports community he or she now belongs to (Serazio, 2013, Voci, 2006).

This new alliance does not mean that the individual will automatically abandon a previous one that may have been developed where he or she grew up. Where someone grew up can also develop a regional allegiance towards his or her hometown team. A young boy or girl who grew up in Texas may be a fan of either the Texas Rangers or the Houston Astros. If this individual moves to Chicago, he or she may become a Cubs fan while still cheering on the Texas team he or she grew up rooting for. Now, a change in location does not automatically mean a change or addition to one's fan choice of teams. Especially for teams that have large nationwide (or even international) followings, a fan can usually find groups who will get together to watch games when available. For example, the Cleveland Browns have a fan organization called the "Browns Backers Worldwide" made up of hundreds of groups throughout the world where Browns fans can come together to watch games, have events, and build friendships through the fandom of the Cleveland Browns (fans.clevelandbrowns.com). This is a great opportunity for social interactions and for fans to generate a sense of belonging.

MY FAMILY AND FRIENDS MADE ME DO IT

Family and friends are major influences in how we learn, what we learn, and our values, beliefs, and morals. Some of these factors also influence how we select teams that we become fans of and those we do not. This does not necessarily mean a child will automatically cheer for the team his or her family is a fan of; sometimes the child will purposefully not do so in an attempt to create their own identity. However, in either of these situations, family was an influence. The best example of this influence is present in the movie *Fever Pitch* (Farrelly & Farrelly, 2005).

Ben Has Red Sox Fever

In the 2004 Fox 2000/Flower Films motion picture, *Fever Pitch*, the audience meets Ben, a teacher and a Boston Red Sox fanatic as he starts a new relationship with Lindsey, a young professional who has never really paid attention to baseball before she met Ben. Though their relationship does seem to be going well, as baseball season starts, things start to get difficult due to Ben's love for the Red Sox. Though the movie does focus on the relationship between the two main characters, the focus here for the purposes of the chapter are more based on the development of Ben's fandom and the growth of the community that builds between Ben and the other Red Sox fans that he spends every summer with as a season ticket holder.

Ben's fascination for the team began as a child when his uncle took him to his first Red Sox game after Ben's family moved to Boston. As the narrator explains in the beginning of the movie, Ben did not have a lot of friends and Fenway was a place he felt excited and at home in Boston. When his uncle passed away, he left Ben his season tickets and, as an adult, the other season ticket holders in his section have grown to become Ben's family. In his perception, sharing the Red Sox with Lindsey is the best way to show her how much he loves her. For Lindsey, the games are events that take time away from her work and, she hopes, up-coming promotion. She sees baseball simply as a game, whereas Ben sees it as family and a way of life. Ben starts to question his extreme fandom after he and Lindsey separate and tries to sell his season tickets, much to the disgust of his "summer family" who do not hold back when expressing their disgust. Eventually, the two are able to come to a compromise, but the show of family and friends' influence on fandom, as well as the expressions of fandom, are a perfect depiction of the sense of fandom and the community that accompanies fandom, as well.

© Joyce Vincent/Shutterstock.com

WE BELIEVE . . .

As the Reysen and Branscombe (2010) definitions of fanship and fandom indicate, being a fan is not just about one person cheering for another, rather it is about a group of individuals coming together for something they see as greater than themselves. This is evident in the "We are . . ." cheers that fill college football stadiums every Saturday, the "12th Man" tradition of the Texas A&M Aggies, a tradition shared by the Seattle Seahawks through their championship run, and the celebration parades held throughout cities meant to include the fans as part of team events (Boren, 2015). If being a fan only allowed people to stay at home and cheer on their team alone, not many would do it. Fans often view themselves, and those they consider part of their fandom, as sharing a sense of group identity.

Expression of Individual Fandom

Much like the example of fandom surrounding New York Yankee Derek Jeter, many find ways to express their fandom through attending games where their favorite player is playing for the away team, purchasing memorabilia from their player, or even clothing from their player's clothing line. Once many in the sports marketing business caught onto the money to be made in the expression of one's fandom, this field began to grow. When Kobe Bryant started his NBA career, he was already a sensation in high school and was drawing the attention of basketball fans nationwide. When he decided to forgo college and declare for the NBA draft straight out of high school, many were sure he would be an early first round draft pick. By the time Bryant was selected 13th in the first round by the Charlotte Hornets (traded immediately to the Los Angeles Lakers), both Nike and Adidas were fighting over who would sign the young future star to a multi-year, multi-million dollar contract (espn.go.com; Petkac, 2013).

Nike was one of the first athletic apparel companies that was able to realize the financial benefit of expressions of fandom with the success of Michael Jordan. The creation of the Jordan clothing and shoe line was also the beginning of the athlete-driven marketing of many athletic apparel companies. Rather than having only the athlete wear a particular style of shoes, shirts, shorts, socks, baseball caps, hooded sweatshirts, etc., organizations realized if they made items specifically for the athlete, fans of the athlete and sport would consume the product at a higher level than non-athlete associated merchandise (sneakernews.com). This led to a new way for more athletes, such as Derek Jeter, Derrick Rose, Kevin Durant, Stephen Curry, Rebecca Lobo, and Diana Taurassi, to make money. Though Billie Jean King and Stan Smith may have started the signature-shoe trend in 1972 with Adidas, and Julius Erving did have the first Converse signature shoe in 1976, the mega endorsement deal never hit the level of money or merchandise available until the Jordan era hit (Bowers, 2013).

This connection to athletic fashion and fandom allows individuals to showcase their fandom without wearing the typical jersey or logo shirt as was the situation in the past. By connecting personal fashion to sport fandom, the clothing and shoe industry was able to take athlete sponsorship to a higher, more socially accepted, and higher income generating, level. Athletic wear, personal identity of the individual athlete, personal identity of the fan, and sport representation all are part of these designs, making them more versatile than most sport-centered clothing. Fans can now show their fandom and fanship in casual and more professional settings.

BELONGING

According to Crawford (2004), being a fan of a team or individual is just as much about enjoyment of sport as it is about one's sense of self-identity. This sense is more about how the individuals sees themselves rather than how others see, or label, the individual. Rather than looking to others to define what it means to be a fan of a team, individuals use fandom to form a sense of self-perception (Wann, 2002). Individuals also define who they are based on who they are *not* a fan of. For example, the New York Yankees are seen as a team who spends money to buy the best players in major league baseball, and therefore a team who buys their championships. This has been the cause of the nickname of "the Evil Empire" (Townsend, 2013). Because of this perception, the fans of the Yankees are seen as "sellouts" and those who are not fans of the team see themselves as purists.

FINDING IDENTITY IN FANDOM

When individuals interact with each other, they tend to not interact with the "person" in front of them, rather they "behave primarily as members of well defined and clearly distinct social categories" (Tajfel, 1978, p. 27). We communicate based on perception and social norms, what we think we know about individuals, and what we believe we know about how to communicate. According to Goffman (1972), we work by rules that tell us when to start and stop communication, we function based on the social norms as to how we perceive our communication partners, which influences the approach we take for beginning and ending initial communication with each partner we encounter. This is no different in a sport setting than it would be for any other setting. When we encounter others who are also fans of a team we cheer for, the inclination is to create a sense of group identity. Kashina, Klein, and Clark (2007) called this phenomenon an **imagined collective** defined as "a collection of individuals who do not interact synchronously with each other and who presuppose the existence of the collection of individuals who share common ground" (p. 35). Just as we see these individuals as in-group members, those who are not part of this fandom are seen as out-group members. This concept of in or out-group membership helps solidify the perceived boundaries of our fandom (Voci, 2006).

Imagined collective a group of individuals who do not interact synchronously but rather assume the existence of the collective of other who share a common ground; a sense of belonging to a group because of a common interest.

SOCIAL IDENTITY THEORY

The core of social identity theory draws from the need for individuals to belong to a group. According to Tajfel (1978), an individual self-concept, or how they perceive their individual sense of value, is often related to the groups they believe themselves to be members of. When individuals find that sense of membership in a group with others, behavior begins to alter and the individual's sense of self-identity starts to mirror that of the social group. This phenomenon can be seen in many different aspects of life, from gaining a sense of family to becoming a member of a school. How often do you see some form of memorabilia adorning your professors' offices that holds the name of the individual's university or hometown? Belonging to something bigger than the individual gives them a sense of purpose and identity.

The concept of **group identification** of an individual is "the evaluation and the emotional components of one's notion of the in-group and one's membership in it" (Tajfel, 1978, p. 29). Sherif (1966) described how intergroup interaction is identified stating, "whenever individuals belonging to one group interact, collectively or individually, with another group or its members in terms of their group identification, we have an instance of intergroup behavior" (p. 12). Tajfel (1978) described three components in the definition of group identity. The first was *cognitive*, where the individual believes or knows he or she belongs to a

Group identification the valuation of and emotional connection to an individual's identification as an in-group member.

group. For example, as a student at the university where you are right now, you identify with the school, the teams, and even perhaps the major you belong to. As a student you will feel an association with the school colors, the words in the alma mater, and the other students in your class. Component two was the *evaluative* component (Tajfel, 1978). This is the understanding that being a member of a particular group could have either "positive or negative value connotation" based on association (Tajfel, 1978, p. 28). The third is an *emotional* component, which deal with the emotions, again either positive or negative, based on either the group, those associated with the group, or both.

The interpersonal and intergroup dynamics can be displayed on a continuum showing one side as the interpersonal factor and the other as intergroup factor. **Interpersonal communication** is the interaction between two individuals focusing on the relationship between the two individuals and the content of the conversation (Tubbs & Moss, 1983). **Intergroup communication** is more focused on the behaviors of the members of the group and is determined by the fact that they are part of different social groups than the out-group members. The difference between the interactions of a pair of individuals versus a group are both defined by the number of members in the group, and are also influenced by group size. When two people are in a conversation with just each other, it is easier for them to relate to their conversational partner on a more personal basis, but when groups are involved, the behaviors will focus on the group and the purpose of the group. For example, if two Dallas Cowboys fans are engaged in an interaction, the conversation may start with the Dallas Cowboys, but could move more to the reasons for their fandom and then to more personal topics. Chances are their behavior will be more fitting for a personal interaction than a group. If these two fans are in a group of Cowboys fans, their conversations may be the same, but might not move to the personal, and their behavior may reflect a group dynamic. Where celebrations between the two may consist of fist bumps and some cheering, the group's celebrations may be more "rowdy" with louder yelling, high fives with others, and maybe some cheers. The expected group behavior will tend to dominate the members' behavior. Different social and even psychological behaviors can be enacted based on which groups individuals define themselves as members of (Reysen & Branscombe, 2010).

Interpersonal Communication the interaction between two individual focusing on the relationship between the two individuals and the content of the conversation.

Intergroup Communication communication that is focused on the behaviors of the members of the group and is determined by the membership in a different social groups than the out-group members.

FANDOM AS AN IDENTIFIER

Sports can provide a sense of identity through either belonging to the team as a participant, or as is the focus for the chapter, as a fan. This also can shed light on fandom of multiple teams within a specific sport or league. Research has identified the constructs of involvement, loyalty, and psychological commitment as independent from each other, or only hinted at the possible cross influences (Iwasaki & Havitz, 1998). Iwasaki and Havitz (1998) also argued that to develop loyalty, and eventually become fans of a sport, team, or athlete, individuals needed to first start with involvement in a leisure activity. Essentially, psychological commitment to a team starts with the selection of one team over another. You cannot like them all, after all. To get from leisure activity to the roots of fandom, Park (1996) stated that one's involvement, in conjunction with their attitudinal loyalty, are both contributing factors to said involvement. Independently they can also contribute to assumptions as to the differing measures of behavior each individual's loyalty.

Often, as in sport fandom, family can play the role of the initial socialization agent when concerning their children's leisure choices (Hoff & Ellis, 1992; Iso-Ahola, 1980). Further, still following the trend of fandom and supporting the concept of group influence on social behavior presented in social identity theory, friends take on the role of socializing agent influencing the choice of leisure activities which then can result in influences in fandom choices. These agents influence values, attitudes, and self-efficacy (Hoff & Ellis, 1992; Iso-Ahola, 1980).

COMMUNICATING FANDOM

When we want to communicate fandom we show who we are through symbolism. **Symbols** are a form of nonverbal communication that we use to help show our identity to others (Goffman, 1958). Clothing, accessories, jewelry, and body modifications are all types of nonverbal, symbolic communication, and all are used by sports fans to express their fanship and engage in fandom. According to Rutherford (1990), the struggle an individual experiences when framing and maintaining an identity exists as a battle between interior and exterior self as well as the battle between one's self and the others around that individual (Porat, 2010).

Symbol a form of nonverbal communication that we use to help show our identity to others.

In sports, fans use logos as countries use flags, to mark their affiliation, and often property as well. Signs may appear on garages indicating "White Sox fan parking here, all others will be towed" or stickers with a fan's favorite team's logo may be placed on cars or trucks. Drive through northern Indiana and you will find Notre Dame logos in blue and gold throughout the area. Travel south to Florida and you will find much of the state split between fans from the University of Florida, Florida State University, and the University of Miami. Showing who we are fans of can take many forms, but the purpose is still the concept of belonging.

DURKHEIM AND SPORTS

In his work on sports fandom, Serazio (2013) uses the work of Emile Durkheim to describe the ritual behind the exercise of fandom. Comparing the gathering of fans for viewing sporting events and celebration to Durkheim's concept of **collective effervescence**, Serazio (2013) explains how gathering in support of a team creates a sense of "social units and reaffirmed group ideals that interrupt the prosaic goings-on of anonymous everyday life" (p. 304). As per Durkheim's analysis, Serazio describes how similar to God being society, the teams are their fans; a team gives their city and their fans purpose and a community to belong to. The emblem of the team then becomes the civic **totem**. Defined by Durkheim as "the sign by which each clan distinguishes itself from others," the totem helps fans identify both who they are as well as others who are part of their clan.

Collective effervescence the gathering of in-group members that creates a sense of the group as a social unit which reaffirms the ideals of the group and an alternative existence to the individual's everyday life.

Totem a symbol that group members can use to both identify as in-group members as well as the out-group membership of others.

Community

Fandom helps bring physical communities together (e.g., cities, towns, neighborhoods) as well as those communities that are not in the immediate location (e.g., distant alumni). As was stated in the introduction, we all have a need to belong to something greater than just ourselves. Fandom gives us this opportunity.

WHAT THIS MEAN FOR SPORT COMMUNICATION

The concept of sport fandom has influenced every aspect of sport. Being a sports fan, as we can generally call it, can influence interactions we engage in and how we engage in those interactions, how we feel about events that happen in sports (i.e., was it good or bad for our team), and what clothes we wear and where we wear them, it can even influence who we follow and engage with on social media. Being a fan helps individuals identify who they are and what they think of themselves. Showing fandom is an attempt to communicate in and of itself; it is a way of identifying with something bigger than oneself and helps give a connection to others that we may not have known otherwise. As technology brings the world closer together, there will undoubtedly be more opportunity for fans to become closer with other like-minded sports lovers as well as the teams and the athletes they idolize. Along those lines, the growth of communication of fandom will too reach levels beyond our ability to currently predict.

DISCUSSION QUESTIONS

1. How are symbols utilized as fandom motivates? Consider team mascots and iconic logos.
2. How has social media changed the role of coaches and/or athletes as gatekeepers of fandom?
3. How can fandom breakdown social issues such as racism? How can it perpetuate the issue?
4. How can fandom breakdown social issues such as those coming up with the LGBTQ community? How can it perpetuate the issue?

REFERENCES

About: 1999 FIFA Women's World Cup. *Ussoccer.com*. Retrieved from http://www.ussoccer.com/about/history/us-soccer-as-host/1999-fifa-womens-world-cup.

Boren, C. (2015, August 17). Seahawks moving away from Texas A&M's 'home of the 12th man'. *Washington Post*. Retrieved from https://www.washingtonpost.com/news/early-lead/wp/2015/08/17/seahawks-moving-away-from-texas-ams-home-of-the-12th-man/.

Bowers, B. (2013, February 7). From Chuck Taylor to LeBron X: Year-by-year evolution of NBA sneakers. *Bleacher Report.* Retrieved from http://bleacher-report.com/articles/1519230-from-chuck-taylor-to-lebron-x-year-by-year-evolution-of-nba-sneakers.

Castellano, A. (2014, September 25). This is how baseball fans have said goodbye to Yankees shortstop Derek Jeter. *ABC News.* Retrieved from http://abcnews.go.com/Sports/baseball-fans-goodbye-yankees-shortstop-derek-jeter/story?id=25752012.

Farrelly, B. (Director), & Farrelly, P. (Director). (2005). *Fever Pitch* [Motion Picture]. USA: Fox 2000 Pictures/Flower Films/Wildgaze Films.

Gottman, E. (1972). *The presentation of self in everyday life.* Doubleday: New York.

History of Air Jordan. *Sneaker News.* Retrieved from http://sneakernews.com/air-jordan-brand-jordan/.

Hoff, A.E., & Ellis, G.D. (1992). Influence of agents of leisure socialization on leisure self-efficacy among university students. *Journal of leisure research, 24(2),* 114–126.

Iso-Ahola, S.E. (1980). *The social psychology of leisure and recreation.* Willliam C. Brown: Dubuque.

Iwaskai, Y., & Harvitz, M.E. (1998). A path analytic model of the relationships between involvement, psychological commitment, and loyalty. *Journal of Leisure Research, 30,* 256–280.

Kashina, Y., Klein, O., & Clark, A.E. (2007). Grounding: Sharing information in social interaction. In K. Fielder (ed.), *Social communication.* (pp. 27–77). Psychology Press: New York.

Kobe Bryant biography. *ESPN.* Retrieved from http://espn.go.com/nba/player/_/id/110/kobe-bryant.

Maslow, A. (1943). A theory of human motivation. *Psychological Review, 50,* 370–396.

Nike signs Kobe Bryant to $40 million contract. (2003, June 25). *The Wall Street Journal.* Retrieved from http://www.wsj.com/articles/SB105649507860753000.

Park, S.H. (1996). Relationships between involvement and attitudinal loyalty constructs in adult fitness programs. *Journal of Leisure Research, 28,* 233–250.

Petkac, L. (2013, February 1). The sneaker evolution of Kobe Bryant. *Bleacher Report.* Retrieved from http://bleacherreport.com/articles/1509138-the-sneaker-evolution-of-kobe-bryant.

Porat, A. (2010). Football fandom: A bounded identification. *Soccer & Society, 11(3),* 277–290.

Reysen, S., & Branscombe, N.R. (2010). Fanship and fandom: Comparisons between sport and non-sport fans. *Journal of Sport Behavior, 33(2),* 176–193.

Rosenberg, M. (2015, July 20). Uniformly bounded. *Sports Illustrated, 123(2),* 72.

Rutherford, J. (1990). *Identity, Community, culture, difference.* Lawrence & Wishart: London.

Schilken, C. (2014, August 18). Joe Maddon rips Rays fans for cheering for Yankees' Derek Jeter. *Los Angeles Times.* http://www.latimes.com/sports/sportsnow/la-sp-sn-joe-maddon-derek-jeter-20140818-story.html.

Serazio, M. (2013). The elementary forms of sport fandom: A Durkheimian exploration of team myths, kinship, and totemic rituals. *Communication and Sport, 1(4),* 1–23.

Tajfel, H. (1978). *Differentiation between social groups.* New York: Academic Press, Inc.

Townsend, M. (2013, February 23). Judge rules that Yankees are baseball's only "evil empire". *Yahoo Sports.* Retrieved from http://sports.yahoo.com/blogs/mlb-big-league-stew/judge-rules-yankees-baseball-only-evil-empire-223119832–mlb.html.

Tubbs, S., & Moss, S. (1983). *A model of human communication.* 3rd ed. Random House: New York. Pp. 23–49.

Voci, A. (2006). Relevance of social categories, depersonalization and group process: Two field studies of self-categorization theory. *European Journal of Social Psychology, 36,* 73–90.

Wann, D.L. (2002). Preliminary validation of a measure for assessing identification as a sport fan: The sport fandom questionnaire. *International Journal of Sport Management, 3,* 103–115.

Welcome to the Dawgpound. Retrieved from http://fans.clevelandbrowns.com.

CHAPTER 8

THE FUTURE OF SPORT COMMUNICATION

Chapter Objectives

At the end of this chapter, readers will be able to:

1. Give a brief explanation of the origins of sport communication as an academic field.
2. List two growth areas for the study of sport communication.
3. Differentiate sport communication from sport journalism and broadcasting.
4. List three communication dynamics that the study of sport communication can help us understand.

Key Terms

Organizational communication	Risk and crisis communication	Social media

INTRODUCTION

The field of communication has grown exponentially over its short, yet influential history. With branches of study and theory development continuing to move the communication research forward, it is only natural for sport communication to be moving along this same positive trend. The move for more specific foci within the core areas of communication studies (i.e., interpersonal, relational, organizational) is essential as sports as an industry and a cultural influencer is only growing. From an interpersonal and relational perspective, as each of the chapters in this book have pointed out, sport and sports participation are both impacted by and directly impact the relationships that are embedded in each.

THEORY AND COMMUNICATION

It is understood that theory is used to predict and explain behaviors, and the use of theory in communication research helps us to understand how and why we communicate as individuals. This understanding has been utilized in many different sub-disciplines and, at the core of sport, it was the work of Nick Trujillo that brought the two together. Trujillo's (1992) piece titled *Interpreting (the work and the talk of) baseball: Perspectives on ballpark culture* published in the *Western Journal of Communication* was the primary piece that helped establish sport communication as a theoretical sub-field within communication studies. Trujillo's work helped establish the groundwork for the connection between theory, in this particular case organizational theory, and the study of sports.

Bringing sport studies into the social sciences was, of course, first accomplished through the research conducted in sociology and anthropology, and later psychology, some of which did include research involving communication. Trujillo's work, however, was one of the first to investigate the influence of social interactions solely from the perspective of sport for the purpose of studying communication. In his piece, Trujillo focused on the organizational structure of a baseball organization, conducting an ethnographic study analyzing nearly every aspect of the culture of the organization. This study examined employee relations from within each department to relationships built across the team. This piece developed as the cornerstone of sport communication as a field, and served as a test for future scholars conducting social science research in the many different fields within this branch of the discipline.

Twenty years later, Trujillo (2012) reflected on the growth of the field, which his baseball study generated. In this reflection from the journal of *Communication and Sport*, Trujillo notes on the presumed frivolousness of sport communication research, and especially as a field, by other scholars in the discipline. The questions posed for why Trujillo would study sports are the same questions all sport communication scholars have faced sometime in their careers. This negative perception of the field represented an overall assumption that studying sport was not serious research, but rather more of an area that scholars ventured into purely for personal interest rather than academic growth. This perception is finally changing.

GROWTH OF A FIELD

This change in perception is due to the increasing number of scholars who are conducting theoretical research solidly grounding sport communication in the social sciences. Since Trujillo's piece was published, communication research in sport has grown to include coach-athlete and team communication based on immediacy, regret messages, and efficacy. Leadership studies based on motivation and cohesion, as well as the more recent move towards computer-mediated communication and the use of social media as a form of the expression of fandom have also expanded the field.

When most individuals hear the term "sport communication" they tend to think of media and broadcasting; however, this is often a misconception. Where those fields are housed in communication studies, they would be better referenced as sport journalism or broadcasting. The differentiation of the practice of communicating about sporting events and the study of sport as a field is crucial to the success, understanding, and representation of this branch of communication studies. It was not that long ago that many, even experts in sport communication, would have agreed with Trujillo (2012) when he stated that he doubted sport communication would have its own specialized journal. This too has changed. The journal *Sport and Communication* ran its first issue in 2012, which has helped solidify the legitimacy of the field to those who doubted its staying power.

THE FUTURE

The diversity of the field is what makes sport communication such an interesting field; however, it is also what has drawn a lot of criticism. The questions from others include "why are these studies important?" as well as "what are the perimeters of the field?". These questions are not difficult to answer on their face. For the question of perimeters, you can simply look to the ever growing influence of sport in our society. As was stated in the introduction, the growth of the sport industry is surpassing that of certain small countries (www.atkearney.com). Between youth leagues, middle and high school athletic programs, collegiate sports, as well as professional sports, there are opportunities for sports to work their way into nearly every aspect of life. The chapters of this book explain how sports can influence the interpersonal relationships connected to sports. As you can tell from the chapters in this book, only half of them focus on relationships that take place on the field of play (group, coach-athlete, and leadership communication). This is because even with interpersonal communication and sports, the influence of sport participation goes beyond the field of play. The other chapters look at these more auxiliary influences, such as the changing of relationships in the family and the fanship and fandom of sports. Beyond the interpersonal relationships that happen in sports, the field is also able to look at several other dynamics in communication.

Organizational Communication

The sport organization is very different from the relationships that take place in non-sport oriented organizations. The similarities that are present are few, such as the presence of a hierarchy, the monetary-based business structure, the rules

Organizational Communication the communication that takes place in and from organizational settings developing social structures and relationships in organizations as well as networks of clients and consumers for organizations.

and regulations, and the need for consumers, just to name a few. However, that is often where the similarities end. In sports, the top of the hierarchy can seem to become more flat as the decision processes within sports are often handled differently than within non-sport entities. For example, in professional sports, the general manager of the team is often the one who makes the final decisions for player acquisitions and trades, especially when considering the drafting of players. Though the head of a department in a non-sport organization is usually the most powerful voice in decisions surrounding hiring and termination of the employees within their department, this is not the case for sports departments. When considering professional athletic teams, one would think that the coach has a say in the team he or she is supposed to be leading; however, he or she often is the last individual consulted. Ironically, if the coach is unable to find success with the team they were given, he or she is usually terminated before the players are traded or the general manager is fired.

Other variations include stakeholder relations. Stakeholders in sports organizations often include sponsors, investors, and fans. The first two are often more traditional; however, the fans can often be compared to product consumers for traditional advertising campaigns. The difference between a consumer of a product versus a consumer of sport lies more in the fanship and fandom aspect, discussed in Chapter 7, rather than need. Because of the seasonal aspect of sports, fan consumption needs to have several components to keep generating income for the organization year-round. This is often achieved through marketing and public relations. Events such as camps, public appearances by the athletes from the team, training camp being open to the public and accompanied by team scrimmages and special events, and the like. A strong social media presence helps with development of stakeholder relations and makes maintaining fandom year-round easier for organizations and athletes than it was in the past.

Social Media communication platforms that use the technological applications to expedite communication to multiple parties for the purpose of networking or information or content sharing.

Social Media

The development of social media has created a new medium for connecting to stakeholders and generating opportunities for public relations, marketing, and athlete relations to grow in a more efficient manner than ever before. Through social media outlets, teams are able to reach out to provide updates about the team as well as about specific athletes. For example, the New York Yankees post pictures of the line-up cards on each of their social media outlets (Facebook, Instagram, and Twitter) letting fans know who will be in the game and who will be coming in to play relief positions. MLB and the NFL highlight the birthdays of their players as well as the anniversaries of record-breaking and setting events via Instagram. The UFC utilizes social media to give information about television shows, upcoming fights, changes in fight cards, and contests. As everyday life becomes increasingly digital, the sports industry has been able to keep up and, in many cases, excel at the use of this new medium.

Athletes, like their celebrity counterparts, have also taken to social media to connect with their fans. This tool has proven to be useful as a means for promoting their teams, sponsorships, and upcoming athletic events. This connection to fans has provided an instant connection to their fans, allowing for a more immediate relationship if the athlete would choose to have it. For example, when UFC President Dana White decided to bring the women's bantamweight division to the fight promotion, fighter Liz Carmouche started a social media campaign to convince Dana White that she should be the first challenger for Ronda Rousey's first title defense. It worked and the first women's championship bout was set. This has worked for other fighters as well. When fight promoters make decisions, records and performances of individual fighters are just as important as matching up fighters that fans want to see. Sports is a business after all, so fighters often rally fans through social media to get the attention of the promoters.

Risk and Crisis Communication

The field of risk and crisis communication in sport is one that is expanding with the recent increase in social issues that are plaguing sports. From concussions to domestic violence, and even to the Boston Marathon bombing bringing terrorism and sports together, sports is no longer immune from the full effects of risk and crisis scenarios. This is not to imply that sports was ever separated from either risk or crisis planning. Common risk areas for sports include athlete injury that could derail a season, attendance problems that could hurt revenue, accidents involving fans (e.g., slipping at the arena, fights between fans, fan illness during games), even power outages during games can be issues that organizations need to plan for. The recent behaviors and incidents involving sports highlight the need for research, planning, and organizational time to be spent in risk and crisis communication.

The concussion issue is one that is not new for sports; however, the long-term effects of concussion injuries are just coming to light. Junior Seau (San Diego Chargers), Kosta Karageorge (Ohio State University), Owen Thomas (University of Pennsylvania), Terry Long (Pittsburgh Steelers) (Carlson, 2014). These men were all football players who committed suicide and later were found to have chronic traumatic encephalopathy (CTE), a "progressive degenerative disease of the brain found in athletes (and others) with a history of repetitive brain trauma, including symptomatic concussions as well as asymptomatic subconcussive hits to the head" (www.bu.edu). This is a condition where the brain trauma causes degeneration of brain tissue and a build up of a protein (tau) in the brain. This condition is not instantaneous; however, we do not yet know a definite time frame for when the protein development or the degeneration begins. CTE has been linked to changes in behaviors including memory loss, depression, and impulse control issues, eventually all leading to dementia (www.bu.edu). The increase in athlete suicides and the connection to CTE have brought about a firestorm of press and medical attention to contact sports such as boxing, where head trauma was being researched as far back as the 1920's, rugby, and of course, football (www.bu.edu).

Beyond concussions, crisis teams have been busy in sports as general increases in athlete problems have been plaguing sports as of late. The increasing incidence of athlete use of performance enhancing drugs (PEDs), arrests for legal issues including alcohol and drug charges, assault, and domestic violence have caused

Risk and Crisis Communication communication that focuses on the prevention, mitigation, and messaging within the theoretical and practical aspects of risk and/or crisis situations presented in society.

teams to have to explain suspensions as well as the reinstatement of athletes who have been in trouble. This is where the connection of social media, sports, and risk and crisis comes to a perfect storm. Where social media is the perfect breeding ground for rumor and commentary on athlete behavior, it is also the ideal place for teams to get information out quickly about the same issues—working to keep the information flowing and doing so in the right direction.

Boston

Terrorism in sports has often been relegated to storylines where teams have rallied cities in need to overcome attacks; the Mets and Yankees playing for their New Yorkers and showing the resolve of the American people after September 11th, football being played after the assignation of John F. Kennedy and moving America forward, even if it was not a popular decision at the time, and the Winter Olympic Games in Salt Lake City bringing the world together to show that terrorism would not stop us from living, again after September 11th. But the bombing in Boston on a Monday in April changed all of that (www.history.com). Now, sport events, just like all others, need to promote safety on a higher level than before. The bombing has changed how safety is considered and communicated to the public. For example, the NFL now requires all fans to use see-through bags in their venues. More stringent security checks of bags and clothing are now in place in even the smallest venues, including metal detectors and x-ray screenings of bags. Sports may still be an escape, but now fans need to be approved for safety to experience leisure.

WHAT THIS MEANS FOR SPORT COMMUNICATION

As the discipline of communication studies continues to grow, so will the field of sport communication. The scholarship of sport can help develop coach, athletes, organizations, and risk management and bring together sports, fans, and communication in a way that it has never experienced before. With the growth of sports as an industry, communication competence in the field has never been more important. Though it was seen as a research hobby in the past, sport communication is now poised to become an integral part of our lives, just as sports has done.

DISCUSSION QUESTIONS

1. What do you see as the future of sport communication?

REFERENCES

A.T. Kearney study: Sports industry growing faster than GDP (2014). Retrieved from https://www.atkearney.com/news-media/news-releases/news-release/-/asset_publisher/00OIL7Jc67KL/content/id/5273085.

Boston Marathon Bombing (n.d.). *History.com*. Retrieved from http://www.history.com/topics/boston-marathon-bombings.

Carlson, A. (December 1, 2015). Former football players' suicides tied to concussions. *The Atlanta Journal-Constitution*. Retrieved from http://www.ajc.com/news/news/kosta-karageorge-cte-football-suicide/njJf9/.

Trujillo, N. (1992). Interpreting (the work and the talk of) baseball: Perspectives on ballpark culture. *Western Journal of Communication, 56,* 350–371.

Trujillo, N. (2012). Reflections on communication and sport: An ethnography and organizations. *Communication & Sport, 1 (1/2),* 68–75.

What is CTE? (n.d.). *BU CTE Center*. Retrieved from http://www.bu.edu/cte/about/what-is-cte/.

GLOSSARY

Active leader individuals take time to monitor group members through the entirety of the task completion process, working towards member support and success as the project/task comes to completion.

Anticipatory Regret motivational messages that express the possibility of regret about future actions.

Attitude a set of beliefs that focus on a specific topic, situation, or object, which can cause a individual to respond in a partisan manner when the attitude is addressed or challenged.

Autocratic leadership style demonstration of more of a leader focused communication style and focusing more on task completion than the growth of the group members in the process.

Beliefs trust or faith in a certain person, idea, or object that one holds important; helps determine future behaviors based on a predisposition of what is right or wrong, or good or bad.

Bonds described as links that people have with their family, friends, and/or culture based on the perception of a shared sense of identity.

Bridges individuals who are considered acquaintances such colleagues, associates, or distant friends.

Causal play more rudimentary activity than sport as it usually entails rules that are common in participation in the particular game rather than a sport across a culture.

Cohesion "an individual's sense of belonging to a particular group and his or her feelings of morale associated with group membership in groups".

Collective effervescence the gathering of in-group members that creates a sense of the group as a social unit which reaffirms the ideals of the group and an alternative existence to the individual's everyday life.

Communication Accommodation Theory extension of SAT that accounts for both verbal and non-verbal behaviors of the communication partners.

Communication allows individuals to create meaning through the coding and decoding of language and nonverbal symbols.

Content level understanding investigates the literal words being used to create messages and what these words are meant to express.

Convergence defined as the behaviors that one individual partakes in as a means to accommodate their communication partner.

Coordinated Management of Meaning a theory which seeks to explain how we are able to successfully create meaning.

Coordinated management of meaning how individuals in a conversation generate understanding in the communication process, which equates to coordination of intended and understood meaning between the two parties.

Counterfactual Regret motivational messages that that look to invoke regret about past experiences.

Culture the communication concepts of shared meaning and understanding within societies.

Democratic leadership style demonstration of a leader sharing power with the group members, including direction and input, as a means to assist in task completion.

Divergence behaviors that one individual partakes in when they make sure to accentuate the differences through their lack of adaptation to behaviors of their communication partners.

Dyadic Power Theory (DPT) a theory that explains just how power can shift from one individual to another in a conversation, often multiple times, without either individual intending to take or relinquish power during the exchange.

Efficacy-

Ego climate the motivational climate where "success is defined in terms of outperforming others using equal or less effort and mistakes are viewed as unacceptable and punished".

Fandom the connection that one individual has with another when each are fans of a particular sport team or athlete.

Fanship one's connection to a particular team or individual athlete.

Formal role group roles and behaviors that each individual is responsible for based on the task set forth and are intended to maximize group potential.

Generation X Individuals who were born between 1961–1981.

Group identification the valuation of and emotional connection to an individual's identification as an in-group member.

Hierarchical structure organizational power structures where every level up the hierarchy is a level up in power.

Imagined collective a group of individuals who do not interact synchronously but rather assume the existence of the collective of other who share a common ground; a sense of belonging to a group because of a common interest.

Immediacy the comfort and/or closeness that are perceived to be shared between the players and the coaches on a team.

Informal role group roles that are not specifically defined nor assigned.

Intergroup Communication communication that is focused on the behaviors of the members of the group and is determined by the membership in a different social groups than the out-group members.

Interpersonal Communication the interaction between two individual focusing on the relationship between the two individuals and the content of the conversation.

Laws-based perspective views communication-based behaviors as more predetermined or mechanical; more predicated on the outside forces that influence behavior.

Leadership the behaviors of an individual responsible for guiding another individual or a group of individuals; the behaviors of a leader.

Leisure often considered free time, though usually time filled with activity

Likert's four systems of leadership the system argues for the progression of leadership styles as needed to keep up with changes in the organization or group.

Linkages individuals who are less than acquaintances, so even further removed from the source and less likely than the other two to provide social capital for the source.

Live modeling involves an individual providing an example of what he or she is seeking from others.

Locomotion an instance where the group is exhibiting the behaviors that are needed to achieve their objectives.

Manifest power power that is a result of an outward attempt by an individual in a conversation to gain control of the power in a conversation.

Mastery climate defined as the condition where "effort, enjoyment, and self-improvement are emphasized, mistakes are not punished but viewed as a medium for learning.

Millennial Generation Individuals who were born between 1982 and 2002.

Nonverbal immediacy behaviors can include behaviors such as non-threatening touches, smiling or eye contact during conversation, or even animated speaking.

Objective ambiguity the lack of certainty an individual has about his or her responsibilities based on factors stemming from the environment or his or her physical state.

Organizational Communication the communication that takes place in and from organizational settings developing social structures and relationships in organizations as well as networks of clients and consumers for organizations.

Passive leader individuals tend to take more of a hand-off approach to guiding group members and group tasks; more incline to engage through final outcome assessment.

Persuasion a purposeful attempt by an individual or group of individuals to influence or change the attitude or behaviors of another or others through communication.

Play associated with a game, activity towards recreational endeavors.

Power defined as "the capacity to produce intended effects and, in particular, the ability to influence the behavior of another person even in the face of resistance".

Relationship level understanding investigates the meaning of and within the relationship at the base of the dyadic communication.

Risk and Crisis Communication communication that focuses on the prevention, mitigation, and messaging within the theoretical and practical aspects of risk and/or crisis situations presented in society.

Role ambiguity a lack of knowledge or understanding as to what their role is in the group, usually associated with the group task.

Rules-based perspective an individual's ability to make choices based on the rules, or norms, that are common in each society.

Self-efficacy one's perception of their own performance during, as well as in the final outcome, of a task.

Social capital identifies what each member can contribute to the group and the other group members individually.

Social cohesion defined as a team coming together to serve a social function.

Social Identity Theory describes how individuals can more internally identify with the group than with outsiders of the group.

Social Media communication platforms that use the technological applications to expedite communication to multiple parties for the purpose of networking or information or content sharing.

Social norms defined as the "rules" for behavior that individuals adhere to based on what they are taught as normal or acceptable for the setting.

Speech Accommodation Theory (SAT) investigated the concepts of association and disassociation through the behaviors individuals displayed in conversation.

Sport game-like activity requiring rules, containing a competitive element, and requiring a level of physical exertion.

Sport relationships interpersonal relationships existing in and/or being influenced by the context of sport.

Subjective ambiguity the information has been delivered to the player by the coach, but the player does not perceive that they have all the information he or she needs.

Symbol a form of nonverbal communication that we use to help show our identity to others.

Symbolic modeling using motivational methods such as visualization to help them achieve the tasks they have before them.

Task cohesion described as the members of a team coming together for the completion of a given task.

Team a group of individuals working together for, or associated through, a common activity or task.

Team efficacy the belief that a team has the skill to complete a given task together.

Theory of Generations the need to combine both time and experiential factors was that to fully understand a generation, one needed to take both a positivistic and phenomenological approach or risk missing crucial aspects of what made one generation different from those before and after.

Totem a symbol that group members can use to both identify as in-group members as well as the out-group membership of others.

Transactional leadership style a leadership style where the leader shares a substantial amount of power with their group members and tends to focus on the end result rather than process.

Transformational leadership style a leadership style that would be placed between the aggressive style of the autocratic leader and the more participative leadership style of the democratic leader.

Values ideals used to help make decisions, big or small, that manifest in specific communication or behaviors when address; are often ordered by importance to the individual.

Verbal persuasion positive informational feedback.

Vicarious experience a process of modeling of experiences to benefit, and perhaps motivate, individuals' future behaviors.

Work activity , usually requiring strength used towards completion of a need or duty.

INDEX

CPSIA information can be obtained at www.ICGtesting.com
Printed in the USA
LVOW09s2008300916

506946LV00001B/1/P